365
Days of Prayer for
Grief
and
Loss

BroadStreet
PUBLISHING

BroadStreet Publishing Group, LLC.
Savage, Minnesota, USA
Broadstreetpublishing.com

365 Days of Prayer for Grief and Loss

© 2020 BroadStreet Publishing®

978-1-4245-6097-4
978-1-4245-6098-1 (ebook)

Prayers composed by Sara Perry.

Design by Chris Garborg | garborgdesign.com
Edited by Michelle Winger | literallyprecise.com

Printed in China.

20 21 22 23 24 25 7 6 5 4 3 2 1

"Pray to me, and I will answer you.
I will tell you important secrets
you have never heard before."

JEREMIAH 33:3 NCV

Introduction

Whether you have made prayer a habit for many years or this is your first prayer devotional, inspiration and comfort is waiting for you in the daily prayers written here.

Prayer is a conversation with God. You don't need to use fancy words or recite long passages of Scripture. Just talk to God. Open your heart. Tell him about your depth of loss and express your grief in whatever way you need to in this moment.

Some days your prayers may be filled with grief, some days with hope, and some with need. Just lay your heart and your prayers at the Father's feet and wait for his compassionate response.

God is the best source of comfort you will find. He knows your heart and he is full of understanding for every situation. Let his strength be yours as you cry out to him. He is listening to every word you say.

As you develop a habit of prayer, think about this:

PRAISE

Begin by telling God how wonderful he is. Focus on which of his many attributes you are grateful for.

REPENTANCE

Before you present your needs to God, pause. Take a moment to examine your heart. If God reveals any unconfessed sin, bring it before him and ask for forgiveness.

ASK

What do you need from your Father in heaven today? Ask him boldly; he is waiting to grant you the desires of your heart.

YIELD

Ask as if it will be done and yield to his will. Acknowledge he may know something you don't or have something even better in mind for you. Trust and accept whatever answer you receive.

January

You will call on me and come and pray to me,
and I will listen to you.

JEREMIAH 29:12 NIV

Eternal Comfort

May our Lord Jesus Christ himself and God our Father,
who loved us and by his grace gave us eternal comfort
and a wonderful hope, comfort you and strengthen you.

2 THESSALONIANS 2:16-17 NLT

God, as I face this new year, I am completely dependent on
you. You are the lifter of my head, and the only true comfort
that settles my anxious heart. When I struggle to hope for
the future, you are the hand that steadies me and reassures
me that you are here right now. You meet me in every
moment, the messy ones and the ordinary. Meet me again
today and surround me with your comforting presence.

Lead me on in your love, Lord, as I cling to you. You are
the hope of my heart and everything that truly matters.
Whatever comes in this next year, I ask that you continue
to guide me in your kindness and the nearness of your
peaceful presence. Strengthen me with your love!

What can you give to God today?

Beyond the Pain

This light momentary affliction is preparing for us an eternal weight of glory beyond all comparison, as we look not to the things that are seen but to the things that are unseen. For the things that are seen are transient, but the things that are unseen are eternal.

2 CORINTHIANS 4:17-18 ESV

God over all, I look to you today. I need your help so much more than I can even express. I feel my strength being drained as I wade through the waters of loss. I feel like I could be swept away by the tides of grief that keep rising around me. Lord, don't let go of me. Don't remove your steady grip from my life. Hold onto me, even when I cannot hold onto you.

Give me eyes to see you in the here and now. I need to know your nearness; even in the pain, you are with me. You promise to never leave me—that's my hope! I trust that even though I can't understand what you are doing in the midst of my suffering, you are at work, making something beautiful out of the ashes.

Where can you see God's goodness in your life?

Called His Own

The LORD will not abandon His people on account
of His great name, because the LORD has been pleased
to make you a people for Himself.

1 SAMUEL 12:22 NASB

Lord, you have called me by name and I am yours. Even in the midst of suffering knowing that you are my perfect Father fills me with peace. You meet me in my mess every time; I don't have to hide from you! Thank you for loving me so completely. I find hope in the promise that you will never abandon me or leave me to sort things out on my own.

When I struggle to see the light in the middle of the darkness of my circumstances, draw closer, Holy Spirit. Surround me with the embrace of your love and whisper your comforting words straight to my heart again. Like a mother's lullaby soothes her child, so lull my heart into peace as I lean into you. Calm my heart again in your presence.

How would you face today differently if you were absolutely convinced that God is for you?

Empowered to Hope

May the God of hope fill you with all joy and peace
in believing, so that you may abound in hope by the
power of the Holy Spirit.

ROMANS 15:13 NRSV

Mover of mountains, you are the only one that can bring
life out of death. Your resurrection power is the same today
as it was when Jesus rose from the grave and defeated
death. I find my hope in you, God, who never changes!
When I can't make sense of the chaos that is stirring
around me, I will look to you. Be my perfect peace that
settles the anxiety of my heart.

You are the one who guides me through the darkest night;
you are more reliable than the sunrise, and I won't lose
heart when you are my constant companion. Even if my
courage wanes and my confidence is called into question,
you don't withdraw and you don't change your mind.
Thank you for your constant presence, Lord.

What are you needing fresh hope for today?

Look to Him

Be of good courage,
And He shall strengthen your heart,
All you who hope in the LORD.

PSALM 119:76 NKJV

Lord, I open my heart again to you today. I know you have the strength I need for whatever comes my way. I'm worn down and tired of relying on my own capacity. My resources are tapped! But you, oh Lord, are never-ending in power. You are flawless in your ability to extend mercy, and you never withhold from those who ask for your help. I know that when I come to you, you never turn me away. You are a loving, welcoming Father and you are so incredibly patient in kindness.

Here I am again, Lord, asking for your help. Thank you for access to your heart that never runs dry. You don't dole out your compassion in small doses. You always give out of abundance, filling to overflowing. I stand under the waterfall of your love today—wash over me and refresh my soul again.

How can you redirect your attention
when you are overwhelmed?

Held by Love

The LORD is close to the brokenhearted;
he rescues those whose spirits are crushed.

PSALM 34:18 NLT

Merciful Father, you see me in my brokenness. When I have no strength to even call out to you, you draw near to me in my heartbreak. I have tasted and seen your goodness in my life, and I believe that I will see it again. But for now, in the depths of pain and grief, you come close and surround me with the covering of your love. I trust that you will not let me be crushed by the weight of this anguish.

Keep me together, Lord, when I feel like I am breaking at the seams. Center me in your kindness. I remember that you don't have any hidden agendas; you love because it is your very nature to do so. I won't hide myself from you or keep you at a distance today. Come in close.

When you are overwhelmed by sadness, do you believe that God's presence is yours in the midst of it?

Help at Hand

Every time they cried out to you in their despair,
you were faithful to deliver them;
you didn't disappoint them.

PSALM 22:5 TPT

Faithful One, you are the same God who delivered the Israelites from the hands of the Egyptians. You led them out of their captivity into freedom. When they wandered the desert, you were with them at all times in tangible ways. You are with me now. As your child, I know that you will not abandon me or leave me alone to fight my battles. You always have a way out, even when deliverance seems impossible.

Right now, I can't see the way out of this suffering. I don't know the way forward. But I do know that you are with me, and you are guiding me. Lead me in your wisdom, and when you speak, may I be quick to listen and put your words into action. You always prove faithful—every single time. I remind myself of your greatness today. Fill my mind with your revelation and my heart with faith to follow you.

Can you recall a time when God answered your prayers?

Solid Ground

He lifted me out of the pit of despair,
out of the mud and the mire.
He set my feet on solid ground
and steadied me as I walked along.

PSALM 40:2 NLT

Father, in this chaotic world full of suffering and trouble,
you are the firm foundation that cannot be shaken.
Your Word is as true as it ever was. Your faithfulness is
unmatched, and your track record is perfect. Where I have
felt stuck, come in your power and lift me out. Where I have
fallen into cycles of despair and coping strategies that do
not serve you or me well, set me on the path of your love.

Steady me in your love, Lord. I know I cannot fight my way
out of quicksand; instead, you are the one who reaches
down and lifts me out. You set my feet on solid ground and
lead me with your steady hand. I won't give up hope as
long as you don't let go of me.

What are you certain of in life?

Shield around Me

You, O LORD, are a shield about me,
my glory, and the lifter of my head.

PSALM 3:3 ESV

Lord, when the arrows of uncontrollable circumstances pierce my armor and I am left with wounds that I cannot tend to, I need you to be attentive. You see what I can't and what others overlook. You see the end from the beginning, and you don't miss a detail. I trust that you will heal every injury and restore every broken part of me. Only you can do that, and I have to believe that you will.

You are so much better than any other love I've ever known. You constantly reach out, check in, and extend your love toward me. I am never found outside of your compassion because it completely covers me. When I am overwhelmed and I struggle to see what you are doing, I will lean into the love that is here with me in every moment. Thank you for your consistent pursuit of my heart.

*Where do you see God's pursuit of you
showing up in your life?*

Light of Love

He has delivered us from the power of darkness and
conveyed us into the kingdom of the Son of His love.

COLOSSIANS 1:13 NKJV

Father of compassion, I am so grateful that you never turn
away from those who call on you. As I offer you the mess
of my life—the sadness, the confusion, and the unbearable
parts—you don't look at me with disapproval in your eyes.
You do not wince with disgust or shame me for the realities
of my brokenness. Rather, you wash over me with the love
of your presence. You remove my shame and heal my pain.

There is no situation too grave or circumstance too
overwhelming for you. You are the deliverer. You are *my*
deliverer. I will be found in you, for you have rushed to
meet me and you cover everything. Every failure, sorrow,
disappointment and longing is enveloped by your love.
I cannot escape you. Why would I try to when you are
life itself?

What can you bring into the light of God's love today?

Confident Hope

Faith is confidence in what we hope for
and assurance about what we do not see.

HEBREWS 11:1 NIV

Holy One, I have heard of your goodness and the ways in which you treat your children. You are kind, tenderhearted, and patient in compassion. You are powerful beyond measure, healing the sick and raising the dead. You are relentless in your rescue, always meeting those who call on you with your powerful defense. You don't turn away a curious heart, and you never require what can't be given.

God, you are perfect in love; meet me with the power of your presence. Change my life so I will never be the same again. I don't want to follow an ideology. Come closer, Lord, and transform me from the inside out. Let my vague optimism be turned to confident hope as you reveal yourself in my life. I trust that you won't leave me to endlessly wonder. You are better than that.

*Is your faith rooted in a system or in
the nature and person of God?*

So Much Grace

From his fullness we have all received,
grace upon grace.

JOHN 1:16 NRSV

God of goodness, you are full of kindness today. I come to you with all of my heavy baggage; this is the time to trade it in for your mercy that brings freedom. I won't hold back anything, for I know that what you give in return is so much better. I'm so grateful that there isn't a limit to your love; I need never hesitate to ask you for anything because you always freely give out of the abundance of your kingdom.

When the storms of life are raging and I have no strength of my own, I come to you, Lord. On the darkest days, your light shines as brightly as it ever did. You are the source of all goodness. Why would I try to find satisfaction anywhere else? Here I am, Lord; fill me again with your powerful presence. In you is everything I could ever need.

What heavy burden can you give to the Lord today?

Come Again

My life's strength melts away with grief and sadness;
come strengthen me and encourage me
with your words.

PSALM 119:28 TPT

Lord, you see the heaviness of my heart and the grief that saps every reserve of strength. When I have nothing to give, you don't require more from me. You come in close with your tender presence, and you surround me with your peace. In the middle of my loss, you sit with me. You are the hand that holds me together when I am falling apart.

My attempts in life to accomplish things with my own abilities fade quickly when the reality of loss hits me like a tsunami. My inner world is in wreckage—I don't even know where to look! But there you are, right in the middle of my chaos, somehow bringing order with your peaceful presence. I don't need to do anything but rest in you right now. Come again, Lord, and hold me close in your love.

When you are overcome with sorrow, do you feel the need to fix it, or do you invite God into it with you?

Learning to Rest

For God alone, O my soul, wait in silence,
for my hope is from him.

PSALM 62:5 ESV

Lord, in the silence, I find that the questions rise more easily to the surface. The doubts come out of hiding and creep into my consciousness. I want to shut them out and pretend they aren't there, but what good would that do? Today, I won't be afraid of what the stillness reveals. I know you see it all anyway. You are not surprised by the thoughts and feelings lurking in the cracks of my heart.

You, God, are full of wisdom. In your wisdom, speak to the unanswered questions that are laid bare in the field of my heart today. I know you won't shame me or turn away in disappointment. You are such a patient, loving Father; you are not disturbed by my uncertainty. I will let the unknown surface and rest in the mystery of your presence changing everything. May hope arise as you meet me here.

*When you sit in silence,
what comes to the surface
of your mind?*

Rooted in Goodness

I would have despaired unless I had believed
that I would see the goodness of the LORD
in the land of the living.

PSALM 27:13 NASB

Good Father, you are quick to come to the aid of your children. When I cry out for help, you don't delay in meeting me right where I am. Though the weight of grief comes in waves, I am still anchored in the stability of your strong love in every tumultuous moment.

Your compassion doesn't despair at my circumstances; your length of love isn't diminished by my heartbreak. I know that in the darkest of nights, you are my constant companion—both when I can sense you and when I can't. You will not leave me to waste away in the dead of night; you provide everything I need to sustain me, and in the morning I will see that your goodness has never left me for a moment. Encourage my heart with your kindness while I wait for the sun to rise again.

When all seems lost, what are you left with?

Unload the Burdens

"Come to me, all you who are weary and burdened, and I will give you rest. Take my yoke upon you and learn from me, for I am gentle and humble in heart, and you will find rest for your souls."

MATTHEW 11:28-29 NIV

Merciful God, you are quick to respond in love. You surprise me with your compassion over and over again as I come to you with my weighty burdens. You never tire of taking my heaviness and giving me your light burden of peace. Partnered with you, I find that you always do the heavy lifting, and you teach me how to live in the tension of peace in the middle of hardship.

I desperately need the rest that you offer, Lord. I don't want to keep trudging on in my own feeble strength. Your way is so much better! I offer you all that has been weighing me down, and I connect my heart to yours, knowing you are always gentle and kind in your leadership.

What has been keeping you from rest?
Can you give it over to the Lord today?

Even More

God gives us even more grace,
as the Scripture says,
"God is against the proud,
but he gives grace to the humble."

JAMES 4:6 NCV

Lord over all, you are the source of everything I need for every situation I face. I know that whatever I come up against is not a surprise to you. I am covered by your loyal love in every moment. You are faithful to supply all that I have need of; in your persistent presence, I find the strength to keep going and the wisdom to step away when it's necessary.

You see my areas of lack, right now in this moment. Holy Spirit, meet me with the abundance of your peace. Empower me and bring clarity to my mind when confusion settles in like a fog. Burn away the mist of misunderstanding with the light of your revelation. You always know exactly how to move and what to say at the right moment. I trust you to do it again, Lord.

What do you need from the Lord today?

Positioned for Rescue

I'm exhausted! My life is spent with sorrow,
my years with sighing and sadness.
Because of all these troubles,
I have no more strength.
My inner being is so weak and frail.

PSALM 31:10 TPT

God, don't turn away from me in my pain. You see the depths of my anguish, and your Word says that you care for me. Come to my rescue and lift me out of the pit of despair that I cannot get out of on my own. I have tried to be better, to think more positively, and to change my habits. All of these things are like Band-Aids thrown on a seeping gash. They cannot save me!

You, Lord, are faithful to come through. I have watched you do it before, and I have to believe you will do it again. Come rescue me and heal my broken heart. Bind up the wounds and transform this suffering into the fertile ground of your redemption work. You are the miracle worker—you are my rescuer. Come again, Lord, and do not delay.

How have you seen God's rescue in your life?

Ask Again

Oh that I might have my request,
and that God would fulfill my hope.

JOB 6:8 ESV

God, I rely on you in every season. Granted, it's easier to trust you when all seems to be going right in my life, but that doesn't mean that you change when my circumstances do. You never waver in love or change your mind about me. I can't even comprehend that truth, but I want it to sink deep into my heart until it's a profound knowing rather than a wish.

I know that you don't grow tired of my asking, even when I do. So today, I come to you with all that's in my heart; I won't hold anything back. You know the depths of my soul, and I give you access to every part of me. I want to be transformed by your relentless love in every area of my life. Fill me again, God, with your mercy. In the waiting, give me hope to hold onto.

What is pressing on your heart today?

My Sustainer

Preserve me, O God,
for in you I put my trust.

PSALM 16:1 NKJV

Father, I cannot pretend that I am capable of lifting myself out of the destructive cycles I so often find myself in. You see where they originated, and you know how to not only preserve me within them, but to break the power of them altogether. I won't despair at my circumstances, knowing that you are strong to save and dedicated to restore all that is broken.

You are the only one I hope in, for you hold the key to every problem. I don't have to try harder; I need only rest in you. So today, Lord, quiet my soul with your perfect peace. Flood my mind with your wisdom that is full of clarity. You are everything I rely on, and in you there is no lack. Sustainer, hold me together in your unfailing love today and every day.

*Where in your life do you need God's power
to break through?*

He Can Take It

Cast all your anxiety on him
because he cares for you.

1 PETER 5:7 NRSV

Holy One, I come to you today with every worry, burden,
and anxiety. Some days they are quieter than others; other
days the noise level is too loud to hear anything else. I
know that I don't need to carry the weight of these on my
own, and I am not responsible to mitigate every possible
outcome in life. There are innumerable unknowns, but not
one is a mystery to you!

Lord, you see the end from the beginning and every
moment in between. Why would I continue to expend
energy on assumptive possibilities when you offer me the
peace of your all-knowing presence? I may not know what
tomorrow holds, but you do. I will trust you, Lord; you can
have all my worries! Give me the confidence that comes
with your nearness. I know that you are with me.

*Can you rest in the knowledge that God sees
what you cannot?*

Help Is Here

From the depths of despair, O Lord,
I call for your help.

PSALM 130:1 NLT

God my help, you are the one I look to when everything is crumbling around me. You are my sustainer in the ease of sunny days and my rescuer when the sky turns dark and I can't see a way out. I need you more than I can express with words; thankfully, you never fail to show up in power. Come through for me again, Lord. You are my only hope.

In the mess of my current reality, I rely on you to be my help and my rescue. I take this opportunity to invite you into this very moment. Holy Spirit, come close with the peace of your presence and settle my anxious nerves. I am desperate for you, but you see that clearly, don't you? Help, Lord—when that's all I can muster to cry out, there you are with your willing support.

How do you need God's help today?

No Need to Despair

"Don't worry, because I am with you.
Don't be afraid, because I am your God.
I will make you strong and will help you;
I will support you with my right hand that saves you."

ISAIAH 41:10 NCV

Lord, you are the support I need in the struggles of life. You hold me tight, making sure I'm not beyond your grip. You lift me up when I stumble and you set me straight when I am turned around. When worries threaten my peace, remind me again of your steadfast love that never changes.

You are more faithful than the most loyal lover and more attentive than the most involved mother. You are perfect in your leadership and your intentions are as pure as your love. I could not find a better comfort in anyone else, try as I might. Draw near to me today with the power of your presence and let hope break through the soil of my heart once again.

What worries can you give to God today?

Radiant Hope

The Lord alone is our radiant hope
and we trust in him with all our hearts.
His wrap-around presence will strengthen us.

PSALM 33:22 TPT

Lord, when I look at my life and see gaping holes where loved ones once stood, I rely on your strength to face the grief. I know that you will not let me be lost to the sorrow that fills my heart, and you will bring me the comfort I need in every bout of weeping. In the dark night of mourning, you are still present in your radiant goodness. You bring hope in the light of your presence, and I will find strength in that place.

Right now, I ask for you to fill my heart with your peace that passes understanding. You remain constant in the chaos and in the calm; when my heart starts to wonder whether I'll make it through this, come in close with your liquid love and hold me together.

Can you choose to trust God again with your healing?

Love Pours In

Hope does not put us to shame, because God's love has been poured into our hearts through the Holy Spirit who has been given to us.

ROMANS 5:5 ESV

God over all, I come to your waterfall of grace today. Wash over me with your kindness and remind me of the steady goodness of your nature. Your unfailing love is my source of strength for every moment. I cannot go on without you. Fill me again to overflowing, that I may have something to give others today. I am so easily depleted these days, so I will come to you all the more, turning my heart and my attention over to your merciful gaze over and over again.

Do not withhold your fierce affection from me today. I need you more than words can express. Holy Spirit, wrap around me the way water envelops matter, leaving no part of me untouched by your peace. You are my source and my strength; no other resource even comes close to your generous grace.

Will you take a moment right now to let God's waterfall of love wash over you?

Limitless Love

Your lovingkindness, O Lord, extends to the heavens,
Your faithfulness reaches to the skies.

Psalm 36:5 nasb

Faithful One, as I recall your kindness in my life—every answered prayer and hope fulfilled—hope breaks through the soil of my heart again. Even in the waiting for your help in my present struggles, I can find your very-present grace in the here and now. Open my eyes to see how big your love is. May my heart expand as your mercy meets me.

As I look to the heavens, my awareness shifts to the greatness of the world around me. My focus is often too small; I can't see the bigger picture when I am focused on one small part of my life. As I lift my eyes, fill my mind with the clarity that a broader perspective brings. Your love knows no limits, and neither can my heart drain your abundant grace. Expand my horizons as I look beyond my limited scope of understanding.

When was the last time you took the time to look up and soak in the vastness of the world around you?

Always Good

The LORD is good to those whose hope is in him,
to the one who seeks him.

LAMENTATIONS 3:25 NIV

Good Father, what a relief it is to my heart that you are readily available whenever I look for you. You do not hide yourself behind thick walls or make yourself the prize at the finish line of an obstacle course meant to test my resolve. When I call, you answer. When I look for you, you are easily found. Your wisdom is not kept in a vault out of my reach or above my position. You freely give your perspective and understanding to those who seek it.

I have so many questions that I've been keeping on the backburner of my mind. Today, I choose to be open with you about everything. You have shown yourself trustworthy and endlessly kind. I know that this time, as with all the others, I will be met by your goodness. May my heart not be deceived by the lie that you are not interested in me; when your presence fills my being, I know that it is with you that I belong, just as I am. You are good, God.

How has God revealed his goodness to you?

New Life Coming

To all who mourn in Israel,
he will give a crown of beauty for ashes,
a joyous blessing instead of mourning,
festive praise instead of despair.
In their righteousness, they will be like great oaks
that the Lord has planted for his own glory.

ISAIAH 61:3 NLT

Restorer, you always have a plan for renewal. You take what is dead and bring life out of it; you never leave me to waste away in despair. You come with your life-giving presence and breathe fresh power into every area that seems hopeless.

Here is my heart, Lord; my life is laid before you like an open book. Come with the power of your presence and do what only you can do—what I can't even imagine to ask for! In my suffering, I know this can't be the end. In my grief, I trust that joy will come in the morning. You feed my soul with the sustenance of your love, and the fruit that appears is more satisfying than I could ever imagine.

What desolate areas of your life need God's restoration?

Everything I Need

"The LORD is my portion," says my soul,
"therefore I will hope in him."

LAMENTATIONS 3:24 ESV

Great sustainer, you hold me together in the incubator of your love. You heal every broken part of me and restore what was lost. Though there is so much in life that is outside of my control, there is nothing that is outside of yours. I know that you, Lord, are not a dictator and that you don't rule with strict law and punishment. There is grace to learn and grow, to make mistakes and to change my mind. You are gracious in your guidance, and you have an abundance of wisdom to give to all who seek after it.

When I look at my life and see lack, I know that it is an opportunity to wait on your provision. You have everything I need, and you won't let me waste away without any options. You are so much better than that. In the drought of life, when there never seems to be enough, you are still there. Your heart of generosity doesn't ever change; I know that you will provide for everything I need.

Where do you need God's provision in your life?

Hope Is Here

I rise before dawn and cry for help;
I put my hope in your words.

PSALM 119:147 NRSV

Holy One, I put my attention on you today. I won't hold back anything in my heart; rather, I come with it fully open before you. When life feels like a continuous drain on my energy and resources, I am discouraged when nothing seems to change. But I won't stop coming to you and calling out for help. You don't turn a deaf ear. Right now, Lord, meet me with the power of your presence. I need to know your nearness.

Show yourself, God! I cannot hope in myself—I have nothing left to give. Refuel my heart with your love and give me the strength that I need for everything I face today. I don't want to keep living with the feeling of failure; raise my awareness to yours and let me see what you see. You do not abandon me to fear but fill me with hope. Do it again, Lord!

When was the last time you approached God like an open book?

Love Covers Everything

He has brought me to his banquet hall,
And his banner over me is love.

SONG OF SOLOMON 2:4 NASB

Father, at your table, there is unending bounty for all who show up. You are the one who has brought me near in the first place; Jesus paved the way to your banqueting hall, and I won't let my invitation go unanswered. Though I struggle to understand the limitlessness of your love, I know that you have welcomed me in to your family. You have not designated me as a distant cousin but a favored child. How can I even comprehend this?

Today, may I see how the length of your love reaches my life. Cover me with your goodness and draw me into your courts where I can feast in your presence again. I am so grateful that you never turn me away, and you don't give up on me when I wander on my own. Here I am, Lord; blow me away with your mercy once again!

When was the last time you sensed
God's abundance in your life?

February

Look to the LORD and his strength;
seek his face always.

1 CHRONICLES 16:11 NIV

He Sees Me

He will not ignore forever all the needs of the poor,
for those in need shall not always be crushed.
Their hopes shall be fulfilled, for God sees it all!

PSALM 9:18 TPT

God, you know every hair on my head. You have counted the freckles on my face and know each crinkle my eye forms when I smile. There is not a detail about me that you have overlooked; there's nothing you've missed. If you know the number of hairs on my head, how much more are you attuned to the thoughts of my heart? I trust that you won't ignore my needs but you will meet each one with your abounding love.

When my heart worries that you will not take care of me, gently remind me of your faithfulness. You have not failed me yet. Even what looks like defeat is turned around by your redemption in my life. I cling to you like moss to a rock and trust that you will not move away from me.

When was the last time you felt seen by God?

Never-ending Help

Do not worry about anything,
but pray and ask God for everything you need,
always giving thanks.

PHILIPPIANS 4:6 NCV

God and King, you are my help. I look to you in times
of plenty, and I look to you even more in times of want.
Though the times and seasons change, you never do.
Here I am, Lord; you see me exactly as I am. You see my
present reality and the situations I face. You see the unseen
struggles and the heartache that I am carrying under the
surface. You see it all.

I lift my eyes to you again and ask that you would come
in power to fill the gaping holes of need I have in my life.
I won't pretend when life is askew that everything is fine,
when you and I both know that's not the case. I present my
case before you, not as a plaintiff before a judge, but as a
child of a good and powerful Father. Thank you for being
with me, as well as for me.

What do you need God's help with today?

Everlasting Life

These things I have written to you who believe in the name of the Son of God, that you may know that you have eternal life, and that you may continue to believe in the name of the Son of God.

1 JOHN 5:13 NKJV

Everlasting God, you have brought me out of darkness into the light. In your Word, you promise that where there is destruction, there will be renewal. You make all things new. I trust you to continue to do that in my life and in the world around me. I can't pretend that death's sting isn't still poignant. The pain of loss and separation from those I love is an awful thing to live with. But even in that, there is hope.

Where you are, there is restoration. I trust that you won't let me be lost to the sorrow that fills me when I remember the gaps that missing loved ones have left. You don't expect me to get over it—that's not how love works. But you do promise to be with me in it. Your companionship is my sweet and steady support. And when I, too, pass on from this life into eternity, there will be no more heartbreak. Restored relationships await. May this be a comfort to my heart and a balm to my soul.

Does the thought of eternal life bring you fear or peace?

Met By Mercy

Let us come boldly to the throne of our gracious God.
There we will receive his mercy, and we will find grace
to help us when we need it most.

HEBREWS 4:16 NLT

Merciful One, I come boldly before you today. You always
meet me with kindness and offer grace that empowers me
to face whatever comes my way. You are the source of all
life, and in you I find that I lack nothing. When my heart
starts to wonder whether your goodness is real, don't
hesitate to draw near in your love again. Your presence is my
best resource; it is the well of everything good in my life.

I need you more than I know how to express. I won't hesitate
to approach you today. I am yours for the taking, Lord;
meet me with your astounding affection that fills me with
indescribable joy. You are so much better than I give you
credit for. If my mind retained your wonder, maybe I wouldn't
so often wander. But you, oh Lord, never grow tired of loving
your children. I'm so grateful that you never change.

*Have questions about God's character kept you
from coming to him?*

Not to Worry

Do not throw away your confidence,
which has a great reward.

HEBREWS 10:35 NCV

Lord, you are the constant keeper of my heart. You have not given up on me, no matter how many times I veer off on my own quests. You are always with me in the highs and the lows, and you don't abandon me even when I completely disregard your wisdom. Your faithfulness is astounding, and I can't begin to say thank you in a way that would do you justice.

Today, I'm returning to you with my whole heart; you can have every part of it. I don't want my life to be dictated by my mood or by what I believe to be right. You are so much better and wiser than that. I bind my heart to yours and my life to you as you guide me through the hills and valleys. I know I can trust you. Be my confidence, Lord. You always prove trustworthy.

Will you give God your worries and hesitation today?

Calmed by Comfort

When anxiety was great within me,
your consolation brought me joy.

PSALM 94:19 NIV

Father, when I am overcome with emotions that feel like they will sweep me away, you keep me anchored in your love. I offer you every worry and stress; I don't want my hope to be choked out by the vines of anxiety. You come in close with your comfort and surround me with the peace of your presence. I will never find another like you who soothes my soul the way you do.

Lord, draw closer even now. Calm me with your gentle nearness and envelop me in your love. There is nothing that I could ever have need of that you couldn't provide. In your storehouse of abundance, you have more than enough resources for every possibility I will ever face. I rely on you more than I can articulate. Who else is there like you in all the earth? Don't fail me now, Lord; reveal your faithfulness in my life again!

Where do you turn for comfort when you are anxious?

Steady Love

Let your steadfast love become my comfort
according to your promise to your servant.

PSALM 119:76 NRSV

Comforter, surround me today with the tender grip of your undivided affection. You are unwavering in compassion and steadfast in mercy. Let this truth sink deep into my being; I want to live it, to breathe it, to embody it. I will find who I am as I soak in your perfect character. Let me be a living reflection of your nature; awaken me to the goodness that is accessible in the same measure every moment through your presence.

When I am undone, hold me together. Love me to life and lead me into wholeness. It can't be too much to ask when you relentlessly pursue me in love. I am yours, Lord—that hasn't changed. You are the hope of my heart, when I feel it and when I don't. Have your way in my life as I surrender over and over again to the tide of your kindness.

Will you surrender your life to the Love that never fails?

All I Need

God will never give you the spirit of fear,
but the Holy Spirit who gives you mighty power,
love, and self-control.

1 TIMOTHY 1:7 TPT

God, you are the source of all that I need. Truthfully, my heart needs a fresh revelation of that to go deep into my soul. Today, fill me with your faultless love that quells every fear. Quiet my confusion with your perfect peace. You see the true state of my soul and you meet me right where I am in every moment.

Holy Spirit, I rely on you to bring light to my heart and mind. You are the wisdom and peace giver. In you, I find clarity in understanding and in trusting when I can't make any sense of what is going on. Don't let me give up hope, Lord, but draw nearer than the very air I breathe. Thank you for your mercy that is always available; you forever meet me with your compassion.

Are you relying on your own understanding, or are you open to God's wisdom for your circumstances?

Deeply Rooted

He will be strong, like a tree planted near water
that sends its roots by a stream.
It is not afraid when the days are hot;
its leaves are always green.
It does not worry in a year when no rain comes;
it always produces fruit.

JEREMIAH 17:8 NCV

King of kings, I belong to you. I have yielded my life to yours, with your Spirit as my guide. You lead me through the wilderness of this life with patience and strength. You tenderly steer me back onto the path of life when I begin to stray. My life is firmly rooted in yours, and the fruit that it bears will reflect the source I'm connected to.

God, I will not fear even in the midst of famine. You are my supply in every season, in every step, at every point in my life. And when do feel distress in my heart, I invite you into it. I know that your love is stronger than any worry or doubt that may crop up. You are bigger than the unknowns of this life; you are more faithful than the rising sun. Fill my life with the fruit of your goodness even in the wasteland.

*Can you see evidence of the fruit of the Spirit
in your current season?*

Not Done Yet

Rejoice in hope,
be patient in tribulation,
be constant in prayer.

ROMANS 12:12 ESV

Almighty God, you see what is before me right now. You know the intricacies of what I'm facing. I take hope in the reality that you see it all and you're not worried. You are full of wisdom and strategies for my life. You are master rebuilder and restorer, and I don't need to fix anything on my own. I know that when I look to you, my heart will find the confidence it's looking for.

My heart falters when I forget your unfailing love and your unchanging goodness. Lead me back to you again when I start to be overwhelmed by tough circumstances. Your peace is always available as my portion, and I freely receive from you today. Holy Spirit, fill me with the liquid love of your presence. You are my hope, my strength, and my shield; may my heart take courage in you today.

When your hope wavers, what is your heart's response?

Led by Love

"I will bring the blind by a way they did not know;
I will lead them in paths they have not known.
I will make darkness light before them,
and crooked places straight.
These things will I do for them and not forsake them."

Isaiah 42:16 NKJV

Lord, you are the light to my path and the hand that steadies me when I stumble. You faithfully guide me through the darkest night and lead me in your love. I am never without your mercy; every single breath I breathe is covered by your goodness. I don't need to fear the unknown with your present peace as my constant companion.

Loving God, I trust that you will not leave me to waste away in my sorrow. You are my strong refuge—a place of peace and rest in the midst of chaos and grief. You will never let me go. As I contemplate your faithful presence in my life, fill me with hope and courage to keep trusting. You are my perfect portion today and forever.

*When you consider the unknowns of life,
where do you find peace that grounds you?*

Perfect Father

You did not receive a spirit of slavery to fall back into
fear, but you have received a spirit of adoption. When
we cry, "Abba! Father!" it is that very Spirit bearing
witness with our spirit that we are children of God.

ROMANS 8:15-16 NRSV

Holy God, your parenting is always done in tenderness
and kindness. You are perfect in your leadership. I am
your child, and you are my Father. I come to you and find
everything I need for everything I face. You freely give
your wisdom when I'm seeking advice, and you rise to my
defense when I am helpless to fight.

In your goodness, I find my place as your child. I don't need
to fear provision or that I need to earn your favor. You are
so much better than the most loving parent. Your intentions
toward me are pure and for my benefit. I yield my heart to
yours today as I lean into your wisdom. Teach me as I press
into you. Fill me with peace as I rest in your loving embrace.
Do what only you can do. I trust you, Abba!

What do you need from your Father today?

Daybreak Is Coming

Do it again! Those Yahweh has set free
will return to Zion
and come celebrating with songs of joy!
They will be crowned with never-ending joy!
Gladness and joy will overwhelm them;
despair and depression will disappear!

ISAIAH 51:11 TPT

Yahweh, you never fail to free your people from what holds them captive. Do it again, Lord. Lead me out of this dark night of the soul into the daybreak of your joy. Your loyal love covers me through every trial and every setback. You never withhold your presence from me, and I know that you surround me even when I can't sense you.

You are my freedom, Lord. Guide me into the fullness of life again. Fill me with peace for today and hope for tomorrow. I know you won't abandon me in the middle of my mess. You are faithful to come through again and again. I lean into your heart of mercy that always flows from a place of abundance. Wash over me, and may every chain that keeps me from your fullness fall away in the light of your love.

Where do you need freedom in your life?

Satisfied Hope

For I hope in You, O LORD;
You will answer, O LORD my God.

PSALM 38:15 NASB

Compassionate One, I cannot stop myself from coming to you again. I feel like a broken record with the requests I bring, but I'm grateful that you don't look down on me for it. I have grown tired with my asking, but you never will. Today, I bind myself to the goodness of your heart again and ask that you would answer me. The Word is full of your faithfulness, and I know that you are the same God today that you were in the pages of the Scriptures.

You are my ultimate hope, God; you never change. You don't have mood swings and you can't be talked out of your love. What a wonder! With your unfailing compassion in mind, here I am. Answer me with your presence. Do not stay at a distance. I'm coming in close; will you press in even closer?

Are you confident that God never grows tired of you?

Forge a Path

Blessed is he whose help is the God of Jacob,
whose hope is in the Lord his God.

PSALM 146:5 ESV

Lord God, you are my help—the only one I can truly rely on. Even I cannot meet my own expectations, but Lord, you always exceed them! When I am struggling to get through the day, overwhelmed by the weightiness of the harsh realities of life, you are there to provide everything I need. You give the strength I lack, the wisdom I long for, and the steadiness of your peace through it all.

Even when I can't see a way out of the mess I'm in, you always forge a path and lead me through. I lean into you today, Lord; I need you so much more than I can stress. Sustain me when I feel the strength draining from my body; knit me together in your love when I feel like I'm coming apart at the seams. Only you can do it. Come through again in your mercy, for you are my God and my help.

*Can you stop trying to hold it together today
and let the Lord hold you?*

Eagerly Waiting

If we hope for what we do not see,
we eagerly wait for it with perseverance.

ROMANS 8:25 NKJV

Lord, you know how my heart has longed for your wholeness in my life. It is so easy to get distracted by the things of this world—the quests for success, the acceptance of those I admire, the longings for more and better in almost every area. But you, Lord, are full of goodness right here and now. You don't withhold your powerful presence from my life until I get it all together. In fact, my part in our partnership is so much less responsibility than I imagine. I benefit from your grace that covers my weakness.

You are the giver of life, and you never hesitate in coming in close with your incredible affection. As I wait for the fulfillment of your promises, I have the best gift of all—you! You are with me in every moment, loving me to life over and over again. Waiting becomes sweet when I am connected to you.

What is the fruit of your life in the waiting seasons?

More than Imagined

Return to your stronghold, O prisoners of hope;
today I declare that I will restore to you double.

ZECHARIAH 9:12 NRSV

God of abundance, you are the source of every good thing.
Your supply is never-ending, and your well of mercy won't
ever run dry. I look to you again. I stir up the hope that has
held me and direct my gaze to your unending goodness.
You haven't left me to waste away in misery; you always
draw near to the brokenhearted and to the weak.

I return to you today, Lord. I come back home to your love;
you haven't withdrawn your compassion from me, though
I have been distracted by the weightiness of the world.
You promise to bring restoration. Lord, how I long for it to
come! You are the hope I long for, and you always give in
greater measure than I could imagine. Don't delay, God;
come in your power once again.

*Do you believe that God will give you
what you need and more?*

Sustained by Peace

You will keep in perfect peace
those whose minds are steadfast,
because they trust in you.

ISAIAH 26:3 NIV

God, my whole life is laid before you; every moment of
it is as clear as day to you. There isn't a detail that you
overlook, and you promise to never leave or abandon me
no matter what. When sadness settles into my soul, it is
difficult to see where you are. In this world, I can't escape
loss or pain, but I can know your peace within it.

Today, Lord, fill me with your perfect peace. Bring clarity to
the confusion of my jumbled thoughts. Breathe your breath
of life over my heart and settle the worries that have been
swirling within me. I remember that you are unchanging and
your love never fails. I trust you, Lord. Flood my being with
your peace like I've never known, bringing rest to my soul.

*Have you known God's present peace
that passes all understanding?*

How Long

How long must I worry and feel sad in my heart all day?
How long will my enemy win over me?

PSALM 13:2 NCV

God of restoration, I set my hope on you again today. In my sorrow, I have struggled to anticipate your goodness in my life. Thankfully, your love is not dependent on my expectations. What a relief! You carry me when I have no strength of my own. You are faithful to meet me with the comfort of your presence when I am undone by overwhelming grief.

Lord, draw even nearer to me today. In my weakness, empower me with your grace. I know that sorrow may last for longer than I would wish, but it won't take me out. This is not a forever reality. Help me to see you in the midst of this and to lean on you as I allow myself to feel the sadness that accompanies the deficit in my life. I trust that you will breathe your life into it again when the time is right. For now, saturate me with your compassion.

Will you ask for God's perspective over your life today?

Constant and True

Jesus Christ is the same yesterday
and today and forever.

HEBREWS 13:3 NASB

Constant One, you are unchanging. In your goodness,
you remain the same. I need this reminder daily if not
multiple times a day! I am so quick to change my mind
depending on my mood, but you never, ever do that. You
are consistent in kindness, always loving and merciful. You
give out of the abundance of your kingdom and you don't
go back on your Word.

What a difference it is to trust in you rather than in myself.
You do not shift or change with the weather, seasons, or
the ages. You are the same powerful, true, loving God as
ever you were or will be. Today, I lean into your unfailing
love that is the same love that delivered Daniel from the
lion's den and Jesus from the tomb. I will never be let down
by your consistent compassion.

*How does what you believe about yourself
reflect in what you believe about God?*

Wait on Him

As I thought of you I moaned,
"God, where are you?"
I'm overwhelmed with despair
as I wait for your help to arrive.

PSALM 77:3 TPT

God over all, I rely on you. I need your help to get through this day let alone this life. When sadness overtakes my heart and I struggle to function, you are the one I depend upon. When grief floods my soul, I know that I need to give it time and space. Help me to lead myself the way you do—in love, kindness, and compassion.

I wait on you to show up in your strength and tenderness again. In my despair, I am quick to think of alternate solutions, but I know that desperation and anxiety is a sign of my fear not your love. Breathe your peace into my fretful heart, easing the tension, when I still don't have answers. I know that you will help me; you don't neglect me, and you never will.

How does waiting make you feel?

Constant Companion

Surely your goodness and love
will be with me all my life,
and I will live in the house of the LORD forever.

PSALM 23:6 NCV

Everlasting God, you are consistent in kindness and lavish in love. I so easily forget your goodness when I am faced with the harsh realities of suffering and pain. I cannot escape loss in this life, but you never promised that. Your vow has always been that you will never leave your children. You do not forsake me in my sorrow, and you will never leave me to drown in grief.

Without you as my constant companion, I don't know what I would do! You are closer than my closest friend and more reliable than my own family. You never fail to show up, and you always have a solution for the toughest dilemmas. I could not find better in anyone else. You are perfect in wisdom, in friendship, and in care. When everyone else falls short of my expectations, I can trust that you never miss a thing. Thank you!

*Are you looking for perfection and fulfillment
in yourself, others, or God?*

Father of Compassion

Praise be to the God and Father of our Lord Jesus
Christ, the Father of compassion and the God
of all comfort.

2 CORINTHIANS 1:3 NIV

Father, I will not hesitate to come to you with the reality
of my heart today. I won't shrink back in fear, wondering
if you will meet me with disapproval or with a smile of
welcome. You are the perfect parent; you never turn away
from your children with annoyance or disdain. You know
me completely, and you accept me as I am.

Though I may question your intentions because of the
experiences I've had with my own family, I know that you
are so much better than anyone I've ever known. Your
love is unrelenting in its intensity, without manipulation
or expectation of certain conditions being filled. You fully
embrace me in every state. You don't expect perfection
from me, just the willingness and openness of relationship.
What a simple and beautiful truth that is.

When you think of God as Father, what comes to mind?

Patient Trust

Be still in the presence of the LORD,
and wait patiently for him to act.
Don't worry about evil people who prosper
or fret about their wicked schemes.

PSALM 37:7 NLT

Lord, you know how prone I am to worry about the future.
When I look around and see evil being celebrated, my
heart sinks in my chest. I don't want to live with no hope to
hold onto. So then, I will fix my eyes on you! You are full of
mercy to all who look to you; you are the defender of the
weak and a comforter to the brokenhearted.

Today, Lord, I will give you all of my anxious thoughts.
Calm my mind with your perfect peace that is so much
wiser than my understanding. As I trust you, turning my
heart toward you moment by moment if necessary, I will
find your steady strength is alive in me. Here I am; have
your way.

*Do you view patience as something you innately have
or as something that can be learned?*

Freedom Is Mine

The Lord is the Spirit,
and where the Spirit of the Lord is,
there is freedom.

2 CORINTHIANS 3:17 NIV

Jesus, you are the ultimate freedom fighter. You laid down your very life in love, and having lost it, you paid the highest price. The grave, however, could not hold you. You raised from the dead in resurrection power, and with it, you broke the chains of sin and death that held us all bound. Jesus, without you, I would have no hope for life at all. I would have no freedom.

As I follow you, and surrender my life to you, you free me from everything that hinders love in my life. You lead me on your path of peace. I don't have to wait another moment to experience the liberty that you have already offered me. Today, Lord, lift my burdens and free me from any fear rooted in my heart. You are so much better than I can imagine, and you are always with me.

In what areas of your life do you need breakthrough?

Not Finished Yet

There is hope for a tree, if it is cut down,
that it will sprout again,
and that its tender shoots will not cease.

JOB 14:7 NKJV

Redeemer, you don't leave anyone or anything without hope. Even when all seems lost, it is not the end. You never give up or give in; you fully see everything just as it is as well as how you'll bring restoration. I will not give into despair today because you are the miracle maker, the King of kings, and the Creator and redeemer of every living thing.

With my eyes set on you, peace floods my heart again. There is no circumstance too difficult for you; you never worry or waver. I have hitched my life to yours; I know you will bring me through the dark valley to the open fields again. I will see where you were breeding life all along when I didn't have the capacity to see it at the time. You never fail, and I will know your goodness in my life yet again.

How has God turned your disappointment into hope?

Never Alone

Behold, the eye of the LORD is on those who fear him,
on those who hope in his steadfast love.

PSALM 33:18 ESV

Comforter, whenever I remember your nearness, you fill me with the reassurance of your loyal love. I can never escape you; why would I want to run away from your kindness? You never fail to calm my nerves with your peaceful presence when I look to you. You are reliable in compassion and perfect in your peace-giving nature.

Even now, Lord, draw closer to me. Remind me today of your close comfort that meets me where I am. Give me a fresh revelation of your goodness. You don't abandon me in my pain or the discomfort of deep sorrow; you won't let me be overtaken by darkness. You surround me with your affection in every single circumstance. Here I am, and here you are; may my soul know your goodness.

*Have you felt the nearness of your God
who never leaves you?*

Still There Is Hope

For You are my hope; O Lord God,
You are my confidence from my youth.

PSALM 71:5 NASB

Lord God, you are the hope that I cling to even when my heart questions whether your goodness really never runs out. In the loneliest valley, you are with me. You always see a way out of every hard situation, even when I can't see past the end of my nose. No matter what I face, you, oh Lord, are faithful, and that won't ever change!

When I think about my history with you and I remember the ways that you've delivered your people over and over again, I can't help but feel hope break through the ground of my heart. When I'm having difficulty seeing you in the realities of my troubles, direct my gaze back to who you are, God. You are wonderful in your redemption power. You have never failed, and you won't start now.

Can you remember a time when God made a way where you couldn't see one?

March

We are confident that he hears us whenever
we ask for anything that pleases him.

1 JOHN 5:14 NLT

Wonderful News

"The blind see again, the crippled walk, lepers are cured,
the deaf hear, the dead are raised back to life, and the
poor and broken now hear of the hope of salvation!"

MATTHEW 11:5 TPT

God of miracles, in you is the fulfillment of every longing.
As I wade through the waters of grief, I know that you are
with me. You have not left me to drown in my sorrow. As
I look to you, may I find that you are working in me right
here and now to bring healing, wholeness, and redemption.

Everything you touch, Jesus, is brought to life. Here I
am today. Touch me with your powerful presence and
make everything that is out of alignment come together
perfectly just as you are perfect. On earth as it is in heaven,
may I be filled with your love that sets everything right.
You never stop doing the impossible, and I trust you to do
in me what I have not even hoped to believe.

Have you experienced or seen God do the impossible?

Lifted Up

Be humble under God's powerful hand so he will lift you up when the right time comes. Give all your worries to him, because he cares about you.

1 PETER 5:6-7 NCV

God, I raise my gaze to you today. I've been so preoccupied with the nitty-gritty of life, and I feel the depletion of my energy. I don't want to go through another day just trying to survive. I need you, Lord—more than I can express. I remember, as I dig into your Word and recall your faithfulness, that you love me more than I can fathom.

Your affection covers me like the warmth of the sun on a hot summer day. I come alive in your love, soaking you in. I will rest in this place today; I will absorb your compassion into my being as you shine on me. I give up trying to just get through and get by; I'm tired of the fight. I know that I can rest in you, and you will lift me up and fill me with everything I need.

Can you step away from the demands of the day for a few minutes to soak in God's love for you?

Dwelling Place

God's dwelling place is now among the people, and he
will dwell with them. "He will wipe every tear from their
eyes. There will be no more death" or mourning or crying
or pain, for the old order of things has passed away.

REVELATION 21:3-4 NIV

Father, there is coming a day where there will be no more
pain and no more weeping. I can hardly imagine that
reality, and even more—I can hardly wait for it. Especially
in the midst of deep grief, the thought of death being a
distant memory is a hopeful one even if it feels far off and
more wish-like than a coming reality.

One thing is for sure: you are always faithful. Your presence
is like a seal of the promises you've made. Come and fill
me with your powerful presence that changes me from the
inside out. Comfort me with your tangible nearness and
love. Encourage my heart today as I open myself to receive
a fresh wave of your grace. Give me a taste of the coming
goodness!

*Does God's comfort in your present reality give you
hope for the future fulfillment of his promises?*

In His Sight

Humble yourselves in the sight of the Lord,
and He will lift you up.

JAMES 4:10 NKJV

Lord over all, you see me right where I am today. You see my present troubles and the state of my heart. You see the realities I'm facing, as well as the stresses that weigh me down. I don't need to pretend with you; I'm so grateful for that. You accept me just as I am, and I won't hold back from you today.

I take this moment to redirect my gaze to you, Lord. You are the same God who embraced me with undivided affection in the beginning. Your compassion never wavers and your mercy never lifts from my life. God, I am yours. Empower me with your presence that I may be filled with your strength. When I struggle to even crawl forward, come and lift me up. You are still my help.

When you run out of your own strength,
where do you turn?

Freed by Love

He delivered us from such a deadly peril, and he will
deliver us. On him we have set our hope that
he will deliver us again.

2 CORINTHIANS 1:10 ESV

Deliverer, I put my hope in you again today. My striving
doesn't get me anywhere; I've tried to pull myself out of
cycles of pain and shame. It doesn't work! Lord, I have to
believe that you—all-powerful God—will rescue me again.
You never grow tired of showing up in love. What an
amazing mystery that you don't grow weary of rescuing
your children.

I would despair if I believed that I was all on my own. You
promise that you will never abandon me in any situation.
Again, Lord, I ask for you to show up and do what only you
can do. Work your miracle power in my life and bring life
out of dead things and restoration to that which seems
beyond repair. I know you can do it.

Is your hope in your own abilities or in God's?

I Am Covered

For you bless the righteous, O LORD;
you cover them with favor as with a shield.

PSALM 5:12 NRSV

Lord God, you are my covering. There is not one moment where you turn away or remove your presence from my life. Even when I cannot sense your nearness, you are close. You faithfully cover me with your compassion all the days of my life. Today, you see right where I am and exactly what I'm facing. Flood me with a fresh knowing, Lord, that you are not only with me but that you are also for me.

Your love is more endless than the drops of water in the earth's atmosphere. You never run out or run dry; there is always a drink to satisfy the thirsty soul. You are my steady hope, Lord, the one who faithfully fulfills all of his promises. Let your favor cover and keep me as I press into you on my most difficult days. Whatever comes, I draw my strength from your presence.

Have you reflected on God's constant presence with you lately?

Renewed Strength

"You were tired out by the length of your road,
Yet you did not say, 'It is hopeless.'
You found renewed strength,
Therefore you did not faint."

ISAIAH 57:10 NASB

God of the ages, you are my rock and my firm foundation.
When the ground beneath me trembles and everything
that can be shaken in my life is knocked loose, you are still
steady. Your love is more reliable than the moon in the
night sky. I know that you never leave, and you won't ever
let me fall beyond your grasp.

God, visit me today with your power and renew my
strength. I've run out of my own, but I know that yours
never ends; I lean on you and not on my own resources.
You are the well that never runs dry, and I drink from
the fountain of your mercy again. Thank you for your
kindnesses that are new every morning.

When you have nothing left to give, what do you do?

My Portion

My people will live free from worry
in secure, quiet homes of peace.

ISAIAH 32:18 TPT

Father, you are the one who steadies me in the midst of the storms of life. You keep me safe and secure in your love, never letting me drift beyond your grasp. Even in the darkest night, you are guiding me with your light. There is nothing that escapes your sight. When I am tempted to worry that I will not make it through, reveal your nearness to me and surround me with your peace.

When anxiety threatens to drown out the clarity I have in you, give me your promised peace that calms the thought storms of my mind. The closeness of your presence soothes my worries. You are the one I rely on because you can do so much more than I could dream. God, you are my perfect portion for every situation I face; with you as my source, I will never lack any good thing at the precise time I need it.

Do you have an area of concern that you can invite God's peace into today?

Immeasurable Goodness

To him who is able to do immeasurably more than all we ask or imagine, according to his power that is at work within us, to him be glory...for ever and ever! Amen.

Ephesians 3:20-21 NIV

Lord, you are full of lovingkindness at every moment. Your mercy rushes like a full river from your heart. When I feel like my heart is breaking and there is no silver lining to be found, you pull me close into your compassion and keep me still in the center of your love. Even when I can't feel you, I know that you are near.

When I have run out of ways to ask for help or the energy to reach out again, you remain faithful to your limitless love and perfect nature. In your mercy, Lord, move in ways that I can't even imagine. Blow me away with your goodness and reveal yourself through your power at work in my life today. I wait on you.

Do you believe that God will move in goodness in every area of your life?

Safe Space

The LORD also will be a refuge for the oppressed,
a refuge in times of trouble.
Those who know Your name will put their trust in You;
for You, LORD, have not forsaken those who seek You.

PSALM 9:9-10 NKJV

Comforter, you are the safe place where I find rest for
my soul amidst the storms of life. You are the peace that
passes all understanding and my true north. With my life
hitched to yours, I know that you will keep me on the path
that leads to life. You are my refuge, Lord, and my constant
source of strength when my own fails.

Again, Lord, I place my trust in you. Every morning is a new
opportunity to yield my heart, my hope, and my intentions
to your higher wisdom and will. My heart's hopes will be
fulfilled in you. Thank you for the reality of your presence
with me now and forever. Your love is my support and the
force that sustains my life.

Are you convinced that God will never abandon you?

Wisdom's Path

Know that wisdom is thus for your soul;
If you find it, then there will be a future,
and your hope will not be cut off.

PROVERBS 24:14 NASB

All-knowing One, you are full of wisdom for every situation. When confusion blurs my thoughts, your truth is the light that burns off the fog of chaos. You bring order to the mess of my swirling emotions, and you set everything in its right place in your higher understanding.

When I see from your perspective, I know that I will comprehend more than I can from my limited view. You see every detail as a part of a bigger whole. Lord, I submit my heart to you again, trusting in your wisdom to guide me into life and restoration. Even when I don't understand the workings as I walk in your way, I will trust that you always lead in love and for my ultimate good.

Do you trust that God's ways are full of wisdom and love?

Not the End

Surely there is a future,
and your hope will not be cut off.

PROVERBS 23:18 ESV

Loving God, today I ask for a fresh revelation of your goodness in my life. I want to see from your perspective and not my own limited view. When I've come to the end of my rope and I can see no way out of the mess I'm in, I trust that you will continue to lead me. If it feels like the end, I know that can't be true. You are restorer and redeemer, and you never give up hope.

I open my heart to you again, Lord. I have no hope on my own. When I rely on my own plans, I know that at some point I will be disappointed. But today I declare that you are my hope, God! You set my path straight and lead me through every dark night into your glorious light. As I walk through the valley, I will remember that it is not the end of my journey. Encourage me as I hold onto you with everything I have.

*What areas of waning hope can you
invite God to guide you through?*

Held Together

He's the hope that holds me
and the Stronghold to shelter me,
the only God for me,
and my great confidence.

PSALM 91:2 TPT

All-powerful God, you hold me together when it feels like everything is falling apart. What a comfort it is to know that nothing worries you; you don't ever get discouraged by the things that overwhelm me. You hem me in with your goodness, surrounding me with your peace that fills me with quiet confidence.

Why would I turn to anything or anyone else for peace when you are the only one who is perfect in love? You don't have ulterior motives hidden in your mercy and you never manipulate or seek to control me. Thank you for your generous love. You are the only God for me! You are the only sure thing in this world; you never change, and you never will. Sustain and heal me in your complete compassion.

When things in life spiral out of control,
do you trust that God is constant in love?

Living Hope

Blessed be the God and Father of our Lord Jesus Christ, who according to His great mercy has caused us to be born again to a living hope through the resurrection of Jesus Christ from the dead.

1 PETER 1:3 NASB

Merciful Father, in you I find true life in the acceptance that you give. You are free from disappointment and not guided by selfish motivations. Whenever I come to you, I am welcomed with open arms of love and mercy that meet me where I am. You give hope when I have run out of all my reserves of confidence. I consistently fall short and disappoint myself, but it is impossible to do with you.

You have provided everything I need in your life-giving resurrection power. Holy Spirit, meet me again with the power of your presence and make me whole in your love. I have no lasting hope apart from you, but in you I find anticipation that is alive, constant, and fulfilling.

When your hopes are dashed, what are the constant truths that remain?

Unwavering Love

The LORD takes pleasure in those who fear him,
in those who hope in his steadfast love.

PSALM 147:11 NRSV

Lord, I know that you are full of love that never ebbs and is always flowing. I turn my heart toward you right now, and I wade into the abundant affection of your heart toward me. I cast aside every fear and doubt that has kept me at the edge of your table, and I take my rightful seat. There is plenty to go around at your banquet table.

My ultimate hope is in your unwavering love, Lord. It is always available; let my heart eat and drink of your goodness again. I need to be reminded of your constant compassion; Holy Spirit, give me a fresh revelation of the goodness of the Father's heart. My confidence is not in myself or in my plans succeeding. My only confidence is you because you never, ever fail.

Where do you see God's consistent love in your life?

All Access Pass

This hope we have as an anchor of the soul,
both sure and steadfast,
and which enters the Presence behind the veil.

HEBREWS 6:19 NKJV

Unchanging One, you are the anchor that keeps my heart in the fullness of your love. I don't need to hesitate in your presence, wondering if I'm welcome. Jesus, your sacrifice tore down everything that kept us separated from the fullness of love. No wall, no heavy veil, no lies, no shame, and no fear can keep me from the love of my God. Nothing can keep your presence from me.

Lord, I haven't found a situation that is beyond your grasp yet even when it looks hopeless on the inside. There is no pain, no suffering, no wrong done or received that can keep your redemption at bay. You are always fighting for me even when I cannot see what you're doing. I trust you today in the midst of my chaos; surround me with your life-giving presence again.

Consider what has felt out of control in your life.
Can you trust that even that is covered by God's love?

All Things with Love

Love bears all things, believes all things,
hopes all things, endures all things.

1 CORINTHIANS 13:7 ESV

God of love, you are the source of my very life. Without you, I have nothing to hold onto—no joy, no peace, nothing that lasts. You, oh Lord, are not just loving but made up of love. When I consider what your love requires, it is not demanding; it always gives more than it takes. There is nothing that is outside of your compassionate and kind grip.

I am held by love every day of my life. With your affection as my oxygen and my lifeblood, I will get through everything that comes against me. Every situation that is out of my control is still subject to your power, and you won't let me be destroyed. You sustain me in the constancy of your presence. You are so much better than I give you credit for. Today, I remind myself of what you've brought me through before. Won't you do it again?

*How has God carried you through
hard circumstances before?*

My Strength

On the day I called you, you answered me.
You made me strong and brave.

PSALM 138:3 NCV

God, I cannot stop myself from crying out to you in my desperation. Just when I thought I had found peace in your presence, the doubts and fears of the unknown crept up to threaten my trust in you. You are constant and unchanging in love. You are not worried, and you haven't given up on me even when I feel completely defeated.

Thank you that it is not my own strength that makes a difference—what a relief! I have nothing more to give on my own. I confess that I don't feel like I can take much more; don't leave me to be swept away by the waves of uncertainty. Anchor me in your love and fill me with courage that comes from the confidence of your consistent help in my life. Don't let me down, God; I rely on you.

What areas do you need courage for today?

Help Me

It is good that one should hope and wait quietly
for the salvation of the LORD.

LAMENTATIONS 3:26 NKJV

Lord, today I quiet the noise of my mind as I spend a few uninterrupted moments with you. I set aside the worries and the uncertainties of my heart as I lean into your love right now. I come to you with the reality of my world as it is. I won't try to dress it up or down, but I will let you into it. Shine in my life with the light of your truth and wisdom.

There is so much out of my control that I just can't get a hold of right now. I am like a top, spinning. But you are steady and sure; you are a firm foundation. You are faithful to deliver me from the chaos of the storms of life with your love. I depend on you, God; you are the only hope I know to have. You are the only help with a perfect track record. I give up my own notions of what should be done, and I surrender to your perfect ways. Come through again.

*When was the last time you quieted your thoughts
before the Lord?*

A Higher Perspective

I pray that the eyes of your heart may be enlightened, so that you will know what is the hope of His calling, what are the riches of the glory of His inheritance in the saints.

EPHESIANS 1:18 NASB

Redeemer, in you everything is made whole. You leave nothing untouched by your mercy and love. I rely on your perfect perspective to lift me out of the drudgery of the day-to-day survival mode that I've been stuck in. You are full of goodness, freely offering hope to the most downcast souls.

Today, enlighten my heart again with the revelation of your abundant grace. When my resources are depleted, there is a source that is never tapped out. Fill my heart with the hope of your kingdom reality—alive here and now and always available to willing and open hearts. Here I am, Lord, open to receive your wisdom that is better than life itself. Like one who has found hidden treasure, I will rejoice in the beauty of your life-giving power that is the fuel to keep me running in your way of love.

Have you ever tried to look at your life from outside of your first-hand experience?

Revelation's Light

Your faith and love rise within you as you access all the treasures of your inheritance stored up in the heavenly realm. For the revelation of the true gospel is as real today as the day you first heard of our glorious hope, now that you have believed in the truth of the gospel.

COLOSSIANS 1:5 TPT

Father of wisdom, you have the solution to every question I could ever ask. You see the end from the beginning as well as every detail that holds this world together. You don't miss a thing. Enlighten the eyes of my heart to see the way that you do. I don't want to stay on the merry-go-round of short-sightedness that leads to disillusion.

Reach out again in your love and flood my mind with the clarity of your peace. Though I may have good ideas, I know that yours are always perfect. I want to follow you on the path of love that leads to life. It is not the easy way, but I know that it will bring the most satisfaction as I learn your kingdom principles are better than the world's ways. In my joy and in my pain, you are the one I trust to guide me through this life.

What are your guiding values?

Forever Faithful

The LORD always keeps his promises;
he is gracious in all he does.

PSALM 145:13 NLT

Lord, you are slow to anger and always rich in love. You give your grace out like candy being thrown from floats in a parade and even much more liberally. There is no end to the abundance of your heart of love and mercy that flows freely at all times. When I forget your goodness, come with a wave of your presence to remind me that you never leave at any moment.

You are faithful in all you do, and you never neglect a single promise that you've made. When my heart dips in distress, show up in your power and lift my perspective to yours that I may see you at work here and now. Do not withhold your peace; it is the calm that settles over my soul, bringing me more comfort than I can express. Faithful One, do not fail me now.

*When your heart falters in faith,
do you trust that God is still faithful?*

My Refuge

The Lord is good, a refuge in times of trouble.
He cares for those who trust in him.

NAHUM 1:7 NIV

Jehovah, your arms are the ones I run into in every troubling time. I can't stop coming back to you because it's in your presence that I find the solace my soul is looking for. When it's been a while since I turned my attention to you, I find that you have not changed one bit. You haven't missed a second of my life; your love hasn't diminished one iota.

It's almost too wonderful, this love of yours. It seems too good to be true that you would never second-guess your generous mercy toward me. When I remember your goodness in my life, my heart dares to hope that I may experience it again. You never leave; I know this with my head, but I need you to drive it down deep into my heart as I experience your nearness again. Even when I hesitate in love, you never do. Here you are again, loving me with such complete abandon that I can hardly take it in.

*When your heart is unsure, will you still allow
God's love to permeate your being?*

Hidden in Love

You are my hiding place;
You shall preserve me from trouble;
You shall surround me with songs of deliverance.

PSALM 32:7 NKJV

Holy One, when the storms of life rage and I lose my footing, there you are to catch me and bring me to safety. I hide myself in the safety of your embrace, trusting that you cover me completely. You see my aching heart, and you don't look down on me for being in pain. You come to my rescue and surround me with the healing balm of your presence.

I have no hope apart from you—no confidence in anything of my own or of the world's. You are the only thing that lasts in this world full of passing trends and inevitable decay. You are the same powerful, compassionate God who delivered Daniel from the lion's den and led the Israelites out of captivity. I trust that you won't let me fall, God, and you will get me through everything I face.

When life gets too overwhelming,
where do you find peace?

Tower of Strength

The name of the LORD is a strong tower;
the righteous runs into it and is safe.

PROVERBS 18:10 NASB

Lord, you are the tower of strength I run to when I feel like the world is closing in on me. I don't have the resolve to fight for myself—and even if I did, my own muscle is too feeble for it. You are God of the underdog, and you specialize in turning impossible situations into victories. I trust that you will do that in my life. I depend on you, Lord, not on myself.

When I am too tired to go on, you invite me into the respite of your presence, where I can rest in your peace. Defender, you are the one who must fight for me. Don't let me be ambushed by the enemy, and don't let me be overcome by the worries of this world. You are bigger than all of it. Do what only you can do and bring victory in the areas where I see no way out on my own.

*Where do you need to see God's hand of victory
in your life?*

My Caretaker

The LORD is all I need.
He takes care of me.
My share in life has been pleasant;
my part has been beautiful.

PSALM 16:5-6 NCV

Faithful One, when my life's energy is depleting and I have nothing to offer, I know that you are still all I need. In my weakness, I come to you again. As I recall the wonderful ways you've been attentive to my cries for help, my heart swells with gratitude. I remember. I remember how you were with me in joy-filled days and in the darkest days of my life. You won't stop now; you haven't given up on me. May I not give up on you!

Take care of me with your nurturing presence that heals, restores, and supports. You are so much more than life-sustainer, you are life-giver. Breathe new life where I can see nothing but ashes. Turn my mourning into dancing again. I need you.

How has God taken care of you?

Fighting for Me

The LORD your God is the one who goes with you to
fight for you against your enemies to give you victory.

DEUTERONOMY 20:4 NIV

Victorious One, in you is every triumph. When it seems
as though all is hopeless and there is no path for peace,
you somehow make a way and redeem every situation.
Someday, with unveiled eyes, I will see it all plainly as you
see it all. For now, I trust that you have not given up or
given in. You are still faithful to your promises.

You haven't failed, and if it looks like you have, I know it
isn't the end! You always come through with redemption
and resurrection power. Always. I hang on to you and
trust that you are fighting for me in ways that I can't bring
myself to ask. I am not alone in any battle. Fill me now with
your broader perspective and the presence of your love
that quells every fear.

*Where you have felt utterly alone,
do you know that God is fighting for you?*

Entwined

Here's what I've learned through it all:
Don't give up; don't be impatient;
be entwined as one with the Lord.
Be brave and courageous, and never lose hope.
Yes, keep on waiting—for he will never disappoint you!

PSALM 27:14 TPT

God, here I am again with open arms before you in surrender. You have seen my heart full of confidence, and you have seen it quake with fear. Today, I return to you with all that I have and all that I lack. Your Word is full of reminders to not fear. I have tried; sometimes I succeed and other times I utterly fail. But your faithfulness is not dependent on my faith.

May your peace that passes all understanding fill me as my heart is entwined with yours. Though the darkness of starless nights causes me to question what you're up to, when morning comes I can see the evidence that you were with me all along. I know that this time won't be any different. You will come through like you always do. Let my heart take hope in you again.

Will you allow hope to rise again in your heart today?

Promises Kept

Sustain me according to Your word, that I may live;
And do not let me be ashamed of my hope.

PSALM 119:116 NASB

Great God, no word that you speak is without effect.
Every promise you make is a vow that is bound by your
love; you will accomplish all that you have said you would.
In the midst of suffering, my hopes feel vain. But you
never change. You won't let me waste away in despair or
defeat; that's not how you treat your children. You give the
comfort of your presence, good Father.

Don't fail me, Lord; you are the hope of my life and the one
I look to in every season of the soul. When I stray, there
you are to pull me back onto the path of life. When my
heart begins to fail, come close with your love. Remind me
of your perfect nature revealed through your Word. Your
kindness will never let me down.

What are your hopes rooted in?

Healing for My Heart

For you who fear my name,
the sun of righteousness shall rise
with healing in its wings.

MALACHI 4:2 ESV

Healer, oh how I need you to draw near again today. I have no strength left of my own, and I feel like my heart is wasting away in sorrow as I deal with the losses in my life. It's almost too much to bear, this aching deep within. At times, it engulfs me, and other times it slows to a simmer just beneath the surface. You see it, Lord, and you don't despise my pain.

Come close, Holy Spirit, and heal me with your love. Where the pain feels like an endless void where I could lose myself, hold me up and detach the trauma associated with it. I see my own sorrow reflected in your eyes and know that you don't expect me to get over this. But you will get me through it. With your love as my companion, I trust that I will know joy again.

Do you trust God to heal your heart even if it is a process?

My Firm Hope

"Let not your heart be troubled; you believe in God, believe also in Me. In My Father's house are many mansions. I go to prepare a place for you. And if I go and prepare a place for you, I will come again and receive you to Myself; that where I am, there you may be also."

JOHN 14:1-3 NKJV

Father, today as I consider the pain of unmet expectations, I lay all of my disappointment at your feet. I know that in the end you are always working to redeem and restore. I ask to be able to see through the lens of your kindness today; I lay down my defense of pride and invite you into the vulnerable places of my heart.

Where I have been keeping you at a distance, I ask that you would cover it right now. Close the gap and come in closer than I've let you in before. You have access to my heart because I know that you are kind and tender. Your love is for me, and all that you work, you do for my benefit. Help me to see where you have been and what you've been up to.

Where do you need a fresh perspective in your pain?

April

The earnest prayer of a righteous person has
great power and produces wonderful results.

JAMES 5:16 NLT

Home in Him

A father of the fatherless and a judge for the widows,
is God in His holy habitation.
God makes a home for the lonely;
He leads out the prisoners into prosperity.

PSALM 68:5-6 NASB

Faithful Father, when I feel alone in my circumstances, you always bring me back to you. You don't leave me to wallow in isolation; rather, you gather me into your arms like a loving Father. You are closer than my closest friend and always so faithful to show up. When my heart is overcome by pain, you draw near in your comfort and wrap around me like a blanket.

I am never alone because you are always with me. Your constant presence gives me courage when my strength and good intentions fail. I look to you for everything I need. Nothing lasts forever in this ever-changing world but you. May I never forget your unfailing kindness that transcends every circumstance. My heart is your home; may I always be found in you.

When you feel isolated, where do you find the comfort of community?

Champion Defender

He alone is my safe place;
his wrap-around presence always protects me.
For he is my champion defender;
there's no risk of failure with God.
So why would I let worry paralyze me,
even when troubles multiply around me?

PSALM 62:2 TPT

Almighty God, you are the ultimate safe place. While nations rage against each other and injustices are committed all over the earth, you won't let any horrible situation go without your redemptive hand bringing life out of the ashes. You are a master of recovery. I know that you will keep me secure in your arms, and even when my heart quakes in the face of impossible odds, I will remember that you are for me.

I trust you to be my defense especially when I have no safeguards of my own. You know exactly how to rise to protect me just when I need it; I don't need to fear with Creator God as my covering! I release my worries, especially the dread that has been mounting within me, into your hands. I won't stop looking for you; you are my stronghold and the only help I need.

What battle are you tired of fighting on your own?

Restored by Peace

The LORD is my shepherd, I shall not want.
He makes me lie down in green pastures;
he leads me beside still waters;
he restores my soul.

PSALM 23:1-3 NRSV

Shepherd of my soul, lead me beside the still waters of your love again today. Guide me into the rest I long for and rejuvenate my weary heart. You are a good and faithful leader, and I don't need to worry that you will lead me astray. Your love always brings peace; how I long for your peace to fill me once again.

When I start to wander off your path of life into the territory where chaos reigns free and the enemy seeks to destroy me, I ask that you would bring me back. You are faithful to do it time and time again. Pick me up if you need to, and carry me back to your safe space where I find rest for my soul. Restore me again as I drink from your river of life.

When was the last time you felt refreshed by God?

Not Far Away

The LORD is near to the brokenhearted
and saves the crushed in spirit.

PSALM 34:18 ESV

Lord, when my heart is broken and I struggle to even find the strength to get through a normal day, would you come in close with your love? When I can't stop weeping to even form a sentence, you hear the message of my heart without hesitation. You don't need me to explain a thing; you already know and understand the depth of the pain I am experiencing.

Be near, Lord. Closer than my skin and bones; move with your compassionate presence in my very being. Layer your love as my spirit communes with yours. You're not far away and I don't need to beg you to come. Here you are with your perfect peace again. Hold me as I agonize over this and love me back to life. Lift the burdens I am not meant to carry and ease the tension of that which I must walk through. I lean into you.

When your heart is broken, can you sense God's nearness?

Rock of Salvation

My God is my rock. I can run to him for safety. He is my shield and my saving strength, my defender and my place of safety. The LORD saves me from those who want to harm me.

2 SAMUEL 22:3 NCV

Rock of ages, you never change in compassion. Your mercy doesn't rise one day and fall the next. You are consistent in kindness and forever faithful in love. You rise to the defense of those who call on your name, and you surround those who look to you with your unfailing love. There is no time limit to your affection; you are better than the most caring parent this world has ever known.

You are my rock of salvation—my only firm hope. Everything else will pass away, but you never will. You who created the heavens, the earth, and everything within them are the same God who will keep every promise of protection. I follow your faithful leadership, and I know you won't stop guiding me through life. When I've crossed over into eternity, there you will be.

Are you confident of God's steady character?

Make It Clear

Don't hide yourself, Lord, when I come to find you.
You're the God of my salvation;
how can you reject your servant in anger?
You've been my only hope, so don't forsake me now
when I need you!

PSALM 27:9 TPT

God of my salvation, I rely on you more than I can express.
Don't leave me to waste away in my sorrow; I need your
loving touch to restore my hope again. Though I have
seen you at work in my life before, in the midst of this
heartbreak, it is difficult for me to see outside of my
present pain. Meet me here, Lord, and encircle me with
your presence. I cannot wish myself healed and whole, but
I know that you are the healer my heart is looking for.

In my desperation, I've cried out for you more times than I
can count. I know that you are with me, but I need you to
do something more powerful, God! Hold onto me with a
firm grip; do not let me go. Show me your likeness as I look
to you.

Where do you need clarity in your life?

Called by Divine Love

His divine power has granted to us everything pertaining to life and godliness, through the true knowledge of Him who called us by His own glory and excellence.

2 PETER 1:3-4 NASB

Holy One, your lavish love is infinitely pure and full of goodness. It is not selfish, it does not manipulate, and it never shames. Your love covers every guilt and every wrong and softens the hardest heart. Your divine power has given me access to everything I need to live a life of fullness in you. Your kingdom's values are readily available to me at every moment through Christ.

I recall today that you always lead in love. Direct me with your kindness, Lord, and fill my heart with your peace. You are all that I need for every situation I will ever face. In you is the wisdom I have sought for and all the clarity I desire. Today, be the light that makes my path clear and the hand that steadies me when I am unsure of which way to go.

Do you trust God to guide you in every area of your life?

Overcome with Peace

"I have said these things to you, that in me you may have peace. In the world you will have tribulation. But take heart; I have overcome the world."

JOHN 16:33 ESV

Firm foundation, you are never shaken or moved. You remain constant in purpose and pursuit. You don't lose interest even though that's the model that fall into in the world. You never do. When troubles arise and storms pick up speed, your love is as steady as it was when you breathed life into Adam's lungs.

When my heart wavers in trust, remind me of your faithfulness. You have been consistent through the ages, and still you are the same. You have not been defeated by the ways of this world—you are so much bigger than them all! Jesus overcame the world and even death. Be my peace in the midst of chaos. Be my tranquility as I learn what it is to rest in your power.

Where do you need God's peace right now?

A Better Gift

"I am leaving you with a gift—peace of mind and heart.
And the peace I give is a gift the world cannot give.
So don't be troubled or afraid."

JOHN 14:27 NLT

God, you are the giver of all good gifts. There is not one iota of goodness in my life that does not have your signature on it. And yet, you are full of so much more than I could think to ask for. You give in ways that the world doesn't know how to. Who can calm anxious nerves? Who can settle a restless heart? Who can heal the trauma of the past and give hope for the future?

It is you. What you give is personal, and it is received straight from your Spirit, with no middleman involved. The peace you give is not a temporary fix; it is the atmosphere of your very presence. You calm every anxiety and bring order to the confusion of my mind. Only you can do that, and when you do, I know I've been touched by God. Touch me again.

Have you experienced the peace of God that brings clarity, focus, and rest?

Always with Me

Those who love me, I will deliver;
I will protect those who know my name.
When they call to me, I will answer them;
I will be with them in trouble,
I will rescue them and honor them.

PSALM 91:14-15 NRSV

Father, you have promised to never leave or abandon your children. I have heard it so many times, but my heart needs the reminder almost daily. As I wade through the waters of grief, I need a fresh revelation of this. You have been my portion of peace for as long as I've been aware of your presence in my life. I won't hesitate today to tell you that I need you more than ever.

I won't weary of calling on you; and even when I do, there you are still. Lean into me as I lean into you and weave your peace into the fabric of my soul. You never demean me; you lift me up and honor me with your favor. I can't even grasp how a perfect God like you would give me the time of day, yet you call me family and friend. Thank you for never giving up on me.

What does God's nearness and friendship mean to you?

Can't Stay Away

Those who go to him for help are happy,
and they are never disgraced.

PSALM 34:5 NCV

God of my hope, you are beautiful in all of your ways. Even in my sadness, the joy of your presence refreshes me. You lift my heavy burden of sorrow and lead me into peace as I cycle through waves of deep grief. You never ask me to have it all together, and for that I am grateful. Your kindness sits with me in the surges of sadness, and you hold me close in your comforting embrace of love.

Your love is like the warm sun; I cannot stay away. I find myself gravitating to you throughout the day like a sunflower follows the path of the sun in the sky. I find unrivaled peace and goodness in you. When others disappoint, you never fail me—not even once. Today, fill me with the reassurance of your presence with me in the mundane of my day. You are my source of life.

Are you aware of God's constant companionship?

A Gentle Reminder

"Come to me, all you who are weary and burdened,
and I will give you rest. Take my yoke upon you and
learn from me, for I am gentle and humble in heart,
and you will find rest for your souls."

MATTHEW 11:28-29 NIV

Comforter, I come to you today looking for rest. My soul
has been worn-down by the worries of this world and the
pain of its disappointments. You see the burdens I've been
carrying around—some like badges of honor and others
like the afflictions they are. I don't want to bear the load on
my own anymore. Here you go, God, you can have them.

I know that you are patient in kindness and that you do
not look down on me even for the hesitations in my heart.
I want to follow you, Lord, and know your peace and
rest as I partner with you in this life. Lead me into your
peace where I can let my guard down. Take care of me in
ways that I've resisted to do on my own. Teach me how
to live like you; I know I will find meaning and life in your
leadership.

What burdens have you been holding onto for too long?

Hopeful

This is no empty hope, for God himself is the one who
has prepared us for this wonderful destiny. And to
confirm this promise, he has given us the Holy Spirit,
like an engagement ring, as a guarantee.

2 CORINTHIANS 5:5 TPT

Everlasting Lord, your plans are good and your ways are
full of peace. I choose to walk in the way of your goodness
with my life. Flood my mind with your truth that penetrates
through the surface of my thoughts into the depths of
the questions that are there. You bring clarity with your
wisdom and hope along with it! As long as I'm looking to
you, I will find the confidence I long for.

You never fail, God. You gave your Spirit as a guarantee
that everything you promise will come to fruition. Instead
of promising to return and then leaving with only words to
cling to, you gave us your Spirit that ministers, teaches, and
comforts. What a wonderful gift; your manifest presence
always available and living within us. Thank you, God.

*Have you experienced the power of
the Holy Spirit's work in your life?*

Set Free

"If you abide in My word, you are My disciples indeed.
And you shall know the truth, and the truth
shall make you free."

JOHN 8:31-32 NKJV

Savior, you free me from everything that would keep me at a distance from you. There are no walls, no oceans, no mountains or deserts too big that you haven't overcome and closed the gap with your love. There is no distance between you and me; in this moment, you are here with the fullness of your compassion and kindness. I will sit in this awareness.

You are so much better than I could dream you to be. Meet me with the power of your presence again and love me to life. Infuse me with your peace, calming every tension in my body and mind. When I study your Word, your nature jumps off the page. You are consistent in mercy, never-ending in patient care, and you continually rescue your people. I cannot deny your compassionate character.

As you sit in the presence of God, will you give him time to speak his words of life over you?

Never Left Alone

Those who know the LORD trust him,
because he will not leave those who come to him.

PSALM 9:10 NCV

Lord, I can't count the amount of times I've come to you with my burdens and cares. It's impossible to know the number of times I've cried out to you for help. Still, you never grow tired of me. It doesn't matter how many times I fall, you are always there to pick me up. Your love never wavers; it's almost too much to comprehend. There truly is no one else like you.

You have proven your goodness time and again in my life, and yet I still go through seasons of questioning your kindness. When I am distracted by the way the world is run, I begin to compare you to a faulty system. Lord, I know that even in this, you don't falter in your affection toward me. You never cease to astound with your relentless love. It surrounds me and lifts me out of the drudgery of hopelessness. You never fail to show up in mercy.

Are you confident of God's love toward you?

Source of Healing

Do not be wise in your own eyes;
fear the Lord and turn away from evil.
It will be healing to your body
and refreshment to your bones.

PROVERBS 3:7-8 NASB

Lord, your mercy remains incredible and your kindness consistent throughout the twists and turns of life. Through the ages, you remain the same. Your compassion is like the sun, rising and bringing hope every new day. Your mercy is like the waves of the ocean, washing over the shores of my heart in an endless rhythm. When I have run out of strength, I remember that you are my source and you never run dry!

Spirit of God, meet me with the power of your presence today. Heal my mind, my body, and my heart with your lavish love that pushes past every fear. There is nothing that can keep your love at bay—you are always moving forward in the constancy of your grace. Thank you for pursuing me in love every single day of my life.

Do you see how God's love pursues you?

Lasting Appeal

The world and its desires pass away,
but whoever does the will of God lives forever.

1 JOHN 2:17 NIV

God, you are the ultimate source of peace, hope, and joy. In you, I know that I have everything I need for life and more. You see me in my pursuit, in my questioning and in the areas I feel stuck. Though I change my mind, sometimes daily, you are as constant as the tides of the ocean. However, unlike the tide, you don't rise and fall. You are consistent in compassion and reliable in mercy. When everything else falls away, there you remain with the abundance of your affection.

Lord, keep my heart set on you, even in the midst of temporary disappointments and heartbreak. You are the one thing that I can rely on in this life. I can't depend on myself in the same way. You are unfailing in your goodness and constant in your faithfulness. Thank you for always being a firm foundation I can stand on.

What are the unshakeable values of your life?

Until the End

"Teach them to obey everything that I have taught you,
and I will be with you always,
even until the end of this age."

MATTHEW 28:20 NCV

Everlasting God, you spoke and the world was formed.
Your Word brought light into a dark and formless space.
You imagined your creation and voiced it into existence.
You formed man from dust and breathed life into dry
bones. You created every aspect of nature and said that
it was good. Your heart was full of kindness and affection
then, and it remains the same today. Even until the end
of the age into eternity, you will not abandon those you
fashioned for companionship.

In you, I have found my purpose, my peace, and my
passion. Breathe your life into me again, Lord, and
illuminate the thoughts of my mind with your revelation
light. Today, refresh me and encourage me with your
incredible and persistent presence.

*Do you believe that God is with you
in every messy moment?*

Through Everything

Even if my father and mother abandon me,
the Lord will hold me close.

PSALM 27:10 NLT

Perfect Father, in you I have found the home that I didn't know I could have. Your ways are better and your motives purer than the most tenderhearted parent. In this world, pain is inevitable. Those I love have and will fail to meet my expectations. But you, God, you never do! You are always better. You don't shame me for the mistakes I've made or guilt me into doing something your way.

You lead in kindness, always sharing your wisdom when I look for it. You offer support in mercy, holding me close in your compassion. Your love never fails. Even when I walk through the valley of the shadow of death, as the psalmist wrote, with you by my side, there is no reason to fear. You have been, and will be, with me through it all.

Do you project unmet expectations from others onto God?

Into His Heart

It is impossible for God to lie for we know that his promise and his vow will never change! And now we have run into his heart to hide ourselves in his faithfulness. This is where we find his strength and comfort, for he empowers us to seize what has already been established ahead of time—an unshakeable hope.

HEBREWS 6:18 TPT

Faithful One, I run into your heart today and hide myself in your love. It doesn't matter what storms are raging around me, you are perfect peace and in your presence is the fullness of joy. When I am surrounded by you and your goodness, my heart takes courage. You will not let me be swept away by the current of fear and anxiety. You won't let me drown in despair. You are the rock that is higher, and you are above the waves of confusion.

I confess that outside of your heart, my own starts to waver. I cannot bring peaceful solutions to impossible situations. I have no way of bringing healing to the destruction around me. But you, Lord, are perfect in wisdom. You always know exactly what needs to be done in order to de-escalate the tensest moments. I run into your mercy. In this place, cause hope to rise once again.

Can you pay attention to God's faithfulness today?

Something that Lasts

"All flesh is like grass and all its glory like the flower of grass. The grass withers, and the flower falls, but the word of the LORD remains forever."

1 PETER 1:24-25 ESV

Constant One, when everything fades, you remain unchanging in glory and light. Your goodness does not have an end; there is no cap on your kindness. If loss does anything, it brings awareness to the limited scope of this life. There is immense sadness in the ending of things. But you don't wither and you don't fade. And you have said that there is eternal life beyond—an opportunity to experience beauty beyond measure with no limit.

My heart takes hope in your Word. In my grief, I am not hopeless. In the pain of separation, I am not without hope. But still, the sting of death is real. Today, direct my gaze toward your unfailing love that leads into everlasting life. Give me a glimpse of what is forever and what will never change. You are so much better than I can imagine, and still my heart longs for more.

How has the pain of loss affected your view of eternity?

Face like Flint

The LORD God helps Me,
Therefore, I am not disgraced;
Therefore, I have set My face like flint,
And I know that I will not be ashamed.

ISAIAH 50:7 NASB

Lord God, you are my help in times of trouble. You are my source of strength when I am the weakest I have ever been. You restore me as I hope in you. I cannot pretend to have it together right now. In fact, some days it's a struggle to just get through my basic routine. But you don't despise my weakness; you give me what I need to get through. And when all I can do is survive, you take care of the rest.

As I see you coming through for me in ways I didn't even know to ask, my heart is encouraged. You keep providing in creative ways in my life; somehow, I find that you have given me more than I need. I know that I won't be ashamed because you are advocating for me. I trust that I will experience the freedom of joy in the land of the living. All my hope is in you.

Are you surprised by God's provision of things you didn't even think to pray for?

Love Meets Me

Fill us with your love every morning.
Then we will sing and rejoice all our lives.

PSALM 90:14 NCV

Compassionate One, meet me with your mercy again today. Fill me with your love in a fresh way. Just like a shower refreshes and cleans, you refresh me with your Spirit so that I am ready for a new day. With your faithful love as my source for all that I need, I have no lack. Let the song of my heart be one of gratitude and thanksgiving today.

Just as the rains water the earth and cause rapid growth in the growing season, so rain over me with your compassion. May your love soak into the soil of my heart and quench the thirst of my soul. You never withhold your waters of life from anyone who asks to drink, so I know that you won't leave my cup dry. Fill me to overflowing today, that your love would flow out of me like floodwaters over the riverbanks. May today be a day filled with your generous love pouring over, in, and through me.

What dry areas of your heart need love's waters
to rain down over?

Light of Wisdom

The teaching of your word gives light,
so even the simple can understand.

PSALM 119:130 NLT

Mighty God, in you is the light of life. I drink up your presence like one whose thirst has not been quenched in far too long. I have been running dry more often than I'd like to admit; sadness has seeped me of my strength. But you, Lord, are an ever-flowing fountain of love to all who call on you. I don't need to beg for my portion; you always give freely and generously.

Lord, fill me with the wisdom of your ways. You give revelation to make your truths evident in the simplest of terms. You have solutions for every complex problem, and your answers are not hard to decipher. May my heart understand and my mind comprehend what you are saying today. As I follow your guidelines to life, I will find the keys that I have been looking for.

Do you feel like God's wisdom is hard to find?

Always Reliable

The Lord is faithful, who will establish you
and guard you from the evil one.

2 THESSALONIANS 3:3 NKJV

Faithful One, you are continually reliable in love. I don't
have to worry from one day to the next whether you
have changed your mind about me. You chose me in the
first place, and you don't change your mind about your
children. I may change my plan depending on my moods,
but you never do. You are constant in mercy, and you
always will be. When my mind wonders whether you will
come through, it is not your wisdom I am tuning into, but
fear fueling doubts.

When I consider your track record, I cannot deny your
reliability. And where I cannot spot your goodness, I must
not have revelation to see it. Give me eyes to see, ears to
hear, and a heart that trusts you. Keep me from falling into
the trap of lies that stand against your character. May I
always be established in your unfailing love.

How have you seen God's faithfulness play out in your life?

Never Forgotten

God will never forget the needy;
the hope of the afflicted will never perish.

PSALM 9:18 NIV

God over all, your eyes scan the earth, and you see every needy heart. You don't miss a detail of distress or celebration; you in your boundless wisdom consider it all. Your compassionate heart is turned toward the lonely and the troubled in their time of need. Your mercy meets the needs of those who look to you for help, and you never let them down.

Today, Lord, let my heart be encouraged by your faithful love that reaches into the depths of my pain and surrounds me. You lift me out of the pit of despair; I won't waste away in the anguish of my grief with your powerful presence imparting peace. Fill my senses with your perfect love that overshadows every fear. Your friendship is the purest I've ever known. I may weep from disappointment with others and the unmet expectations that come along, but you, faithful Father, will never let me down or push me away. What a comfort I've found in you.

How does it feel to know that God does not overlook anything in your life?

All Seen

In hope we have been saved, but hope that is seen is
not hope; for who hopes for what he already sees.

ROMANS 8:24 NASB

Lord, all of my longings are filled in you. There is not one
piece that finds its rightful place outside of your loving
hands. I submit every desire to you again—the ones that
ache deeply and the ones floating near the surface of
my heart. You see them all. May my heart be rooted and
grounded in your goodness, trusting that the fruit that
grows will be evidence of your faithful love feeding the
depths that no one can see.

You are endlessly good God; let my heart recount your
mercy in my life and be encouraged today. You are so
much better than my own plans, and your strategies take
everything into account—much more than I could ever see.
Thank you for your grace that leads me in every season:
through the tragic, the ordinary, and the spectacular. You
are there through it all. I bind my heart again to yours and
ask for your presence to bolster my faith.

What are your biggest hopes in life?

Great Acceptance

"The Spirit of the LORD is upon me, and he has anointed me to be hope for the poor, freedom for the brokenhearted, and new eyes for the blind, and to preach to prisoners, 'You are set free!' I have come to share the message of Jubilee, for the time of God's great acceptance has begun."

LUKE 4:18-19 TPT

Spirit of God, I welcome your tangible presence to flood my mind with your revelation light today. Fill my heart with hope that holds onto your goodness and mercy as its measuring stick. Give me eyes to see what you are already doing in my life, and ears to hear what you are saying over every relationship and circumstance. In areas where I have been stuck, give me your perspective to watch as you demolish walls, lift me out of sticky places, and make a straight path through the hard spots.

May every area that is screaming for restoration find it. Breathe your peace over my life and bring redemption to the barren places. I am grateful to be known by you and loved to my core. You don't just tolerate me, you actually enjoy me. May my heart find rest in your delight again. You are so good.

*What areas of your life are desperate
for God's restoring touch?*

He Is Powerful

"Let us praise the Lord, the God of Israel, because he has come to help his people and has given them freedom. He has given us a powerful Savior."

LUKE 1:68-69 NCV

Mighty God, you always come to the aid of your people; you are their help in times of need. Look at my life, Lord, and see how I need your help. Where I have been stuck in coping cycles as I walk through this grief, would you show me a better way to heal? What once served me well no longer works for my growth. I need your wisdom and leadership to show me how to continue to grieve well and press into you for the healing I rely on you for.

Don't let me be washed into the tumultuous deep of the sea of sorrow; may your love be the anchor that grounds me and keeps me from being swept beyond your grasp. I am so thankful for your mercy that keeps me close; you're never far away. You are with me through everything, and I trust that you always will be. Reveal your power in my life today in a real way. Do what only you can do.

Is there something you need help from God to break free from?

Worth My Trust

The LORD is for me; he will help me.
I will look in triumph at those who hate me.
It is better to take refuge in the LORD
than to trust in people.

PSALM 118:7-8 NLT

Loyal Lord, I'm relying on you to help me. You see my struggles today, and they're too much for me to handle on my own. When I try to fix things and find that I'm in a bigger mess than before, I throw my hands up in surrender. Instead of just giving up, Lord, I let go. Come into this mess and bring your peace that clarifies. You are wiser than I am, and you have infinite resources at your disposal. With your help as my hope, I lean on you. I'm done depending on my own understanding. It may get me so far, but it never follows all the way through.

In your power, Lord, do what only you know how to do and bring new life out of the ashes of devastation. I don't even know where to start; I've done all I can. I trust you because you are trustworthy. You are faithful in follow-through; I'm giving in and resting in you today!

*What areas can you trust God with
that are out of your control?*

May

I pray that your hearts will be flooded with light so that you can understand the confident hope he has given to those he called—his holy people who are his rich and glorious inheritance.

EPHESIANS 1:18 NLT

Don't Turn Away

O LORD; give ear to my pleas for mercy!
In your faithfulness answer me, in your righteousness!

PSALM 143:1 ESV

Lord, you are the one I look to for help in every tough situation. I don't want to be stuck in worry or paralyzed by fear that keeps me from moving forward. You see that I am trying; sometimes, I have no reserves left to take another step. Meet me where I am today. Guide me in your goodness still.

You are the restorer, and I need you to repair what is broken in my life. There are wounds that I cannot tend to on my own. I've tried, and the pain of them are as constant as the trickle of a leaky faucet. Heal me, Lord, with your love. Cover me with your faithfulness and lead me back into life. Where my energy has been on a consistent drain, patch the holes of my soul and fill me with your peace.

When you have no grace left to give, what do you do?

Comforting Words

The precepts of the LORD are right,
giving joy to the heart.
The commands of the LORD are radiant,
giving light to the eyes.

PSALM 19:8 NIV

Lord God, your guiding principles are perfect, and your instructions always come from a full heart of love. When I remember that you are for me and my good, as well as for the benefit of those around me, I can trust that your teachings are pure and right. As I follow your ways of love, I will find the peace and joy that I long for deep within. Your insight is radiant with hope and will never lead me astray.

Today, I will look to your words of wisdom for direction. I will align my actions with the fruit of your Spirit, which you make abundantly clear in your Word. Where fear has kept me stagnant, your love leads me in freedom. When I don't know which way to go or what decision to make, I will look to you. It is in this place that I will find the keys for life that will enlighten me to make insightful choices.

*When you are trying to make a decision,
what is your process?*

Hand of Mercy

You in Your mercy have led forth the people
whom You have redeemed;
You have guided them in Your strength
to Your holy habitation.

EXODUS 15:13 NKJV

Redeemer, in your mercy you lead me into your love time and
again. You take me from the ashes of the hardest situations
and bring me into your safe place where you heal and
restore. When you touch my life, there is always evidence
of it. Your kindness is unmistakable, and your goodness is
undeniable. You are the pathway of peace, and an ever-
present help in times of trouble. You are the Lord, and I am
your dearly loved child. I won't be afraid of what tomorrow
will bring because you are with me in every moment.

In your strength, you will continue to guide me all the days
of my life until I am with you in the fullness of your glory, at
home in your holy habitation. May my heart stay connected
to yours in every difficulty. In unbearable pain, you carry
me along in your compassion. You are so good.

Where have you seen God's hand of mercy on your life?

Feet of Jesus

Come, let us bow down in worship,
let us kneel before the LORD our Maker.

PSALM 95:6 NIV

Loving Lord, I bring all that I am before you again today. Here I am, laid out like an open book before you. I humble myself in your presence; my heart longs to be met by your love once more. I honor you and all that you've done in my life up until now. I remember your faithfulness as I look back on my life with the lens of loving perspective. You may not always move how I expect you to—in fact, you rarely do—but you do always come through. You often weave things together more wonderfully than I could imagine.

With the past in mind, I bring myself back into the present with you. Fill my heart with courage as I soak in your mercy and grace anew. Saturate me in your kindness and peace. You are so much greater than I can envision. I long for the day when I'll see you face to face.

What happens in your heart when you humbly offer your attention to God?

Always Learning

Wise people can also listen and learn;
even they can find good advice in these words.

PROVERBS 1:5 NCV

Holy One, I know that there is no end to your limitless
love. Your compassion can be traced back through time,
but even then, who can find its beginning? You are faithful
in kindness and always lead your people in wisdom.
Today, I ask for a fresh dose of your insight. Speak into
the areas of my heart that require it the most. I need your
understanding; I want to see from your broad perspective,
not my limited one.

As I look to you, let me see the bigger picture. Where
I have been hyper-focused on the painful parts of my
life, I ask that you would direct my gaze to where your
mercy is. You provide a perfect portion of peace for every
circumstance in my life. Why would I rely on my own
knowledge when you have all wisdom to offer?

What have you been trying to figure out on your own?

Great Expectation

All praise to God, the Father of our Lord Jesus Christ. It is by his great mercy that we have been born again, because God raised Jesus Christ from the dead. Now we live with great expectation.

1 PETER 1:3 NLT

Hope of the nations, you are the fulfillment of the longing of every heart. You did not leave your people to struggle and strive through this life on their own; neither do you leave me. You have said that you will never leave or abandon your people. As your child, I hold onto this promise like a thirsty soul to a source of fresh water. You are the living water that washes over me, making me pure and not lacking any good thing.

Lord, how I long to see your goodness revealed in my present circumstances. Knit my heart together with yours, that your love would be stitched into my being. My great expectation isn't my deliverance, though you are faithful to deliver. My great expectation is in your faithfulness in all aspects; you are better than anything I could wrap my hands around. Fill me again with hope.

What is your greatest hope in life?

Good Father

"Don't worry. For your Father cares deeply
about even the smallest detail of your life."

MATTHEW 10:30-31 TPT

Faithful Father, you never miss a detail in your loving care.
You don't overlook a thing when you weave our lives
together with the thread of your unfailing love. You are
more creative than the most cutting-edge artist, and you
never run out of resources or ideas. Your solutions cannot
be overstated; you are perfect in your wisdom.

I am desperate for your wisdom in my life. I need
breakthrough in my life that I know only you can give.
Come with a fresh wave of your powerful presence and
bring together in beautiful order what looks like messy
chaos to my eyes. Don't leave a detail untouched. As I see
your fingerprint of mercy in the smallest aspects of my life,
my confidence will continue to grow in your watchful and
tender care over every element. I depend on you.

*What details of your life have been
clearly taken care of by God?*

More Mercy

Do not, O Lord, withhold your mercy from me;
let your steadfast love and your faithfulness
keep me safe forever.

PSALM 40:11 NRSV

Lord, you are merciful in all your ways. There is not one day where I am outside the gates of your compassion. What an amazing thought, that I could never outrun your love. Surround me with comfort again today as my heart swells and dips with hope.

Whether or not I feel it at the moment, I know that your kindness never wavers. You are not furious with me one moment and gentle the next. You are constant in love. Let that truth go deep into the recesses of my heart, past my outer awareness. May your love be the nutrient that feeds the root system of my being, causing me to grow and flourish. You are my source, Lord; I look to you again today. Meet me with your mercy and revive my weak heart.

*When was the last time you felt the warmth
of God's love and acceptance?*

Carried by Grace

In all their affliction He was afflicted,
And the angel of His presence saved them;
In His love and in His mercy He redeemed them,
And He lifted them and carried them all the days of old.

ISAIAH 63:9 NASB

Holy God, you have been my help ever since I first came alive in your love. You drew me into your heart with kindness and washed over me with your mercy that cleansed me from all my sin. You haven't changed your mind about me in the time since, though my heart has wondered and wavered at times. You remain faithful when I am struggling to hold onto any lasting hope.

Come again, Lord, and save me. You see what I'm facing and the torment that my soul has been in. You said that you would never forsake your children; you said that you would not remove your hand of mercy from them. I rely on your love to free me from all my fears. I don't want to waste away under the weight of the pain that threatens to crush my confidence in you. I know that you have not changed, so change my heart that I might trust in you completely.

Have you grown tired of trying to remain hopeful?

In Perfect Faithfulness

LORD, you are my God;
I will exalt you and praise your name,
for in perfect faithfulness
you have done wonderful things,
things planned long ago.

ISAIAH 25:1 NIV

Lord God, your dependability outshines every other. No one can match your devotion, even if they spent every moment of their miniscule lives trying to do so. You are more loyal than the most devout husband, and tenderer than the most caring mother. Though I have understood this in small measure, I constantly need reminding of who you are. In this fast-paced world full of information at my fingertips, I am quick to forget what truly matters in favor of instant gratification.

You, Lord, are all about playing the long game. You know what you are doing, and you are always working in ways that have lasting effects, not just for the short term. May my heart be filled with awe today as you reveal your unmatched goodness with your revelation light once again. Pour your peace into my mind as I set my attention on you. You are always so near.

How often do you think about God's faithfulness in your life?

Kindness Given

The LORD God is like a sun and shield;
the LORD gives us kindness and honor.
He does not hold back anything good
from those whose lives are innocent.

PSALM 84:11 NCV

Kind God, you are so patient in love. You never turn me away when I come to you. Like the prodigal son, who returned home in disgrace and shame, I sometimes cannot even bear the thought of what you must think of me. In my pain, I do not always choose wisely. You are always about loving restoration. Like the father of the prodigal son, you run to meet me at the first sign of my turning. I know that you don't ever turn away from me, even when I turn away from you.

Wash over me with your mercy once again. I am overcome by the reality of your love closing in around me like an incubator of life. You never withhold goodness from my life; I trust that in the darkness, pain, and destruction you will bring beauty out of the ashes. You will cause loveliness to grow out of the barrenness. Give me eyes to see you at work.

*Have you been keeping your distance
from the Lord in any areas?*

Calm My Soul

He awoke and rebuked the wind and said to the sea,
"Peace! Be still!" And the wind ceased,
and there was a great calm.

MARK 4:39 ESV

Peace giver, you speak and the turbulent waves become still. You see the storm that I have been riding out, sometimes just holding on for dear life. I need your peace to settle the seas of my life. I rely on you, Lord; you know how I've tried to fix it but nothing has worked. You are full of wisdom to all who look for it. Here I am, looking for your perfect perspective in my life. Don't fail me now.

Lord, when the winds are still whipping around me, be the peace that soothes my soul. Fill me with the confidence of your persistent love that always brings about goodness. I know that your faithfulness isn't dependent upon my own belief, and I am so grateful for that. Come again. Bring calm to the chaos and order to the bedlam of my life.

When life is messy, where do you find calm?

Truth that Remains

The very essence of your words is truth;
all your just regulations will stand forever.

PSALM 119:160

Father of all, you speak and the earth responds. You set
your intentions and everything aligns to it. Today, would
you fill me with the wisdom that comes from seeing
from your perspective? I have grown weary of my own
understanding; it's so limited. I cannot see the way that you
will work everything out in my life, but I have to hope that
you will do it. You are reliable in mercy and always leading
in kindness.

In your light, I will see what is impossible to see on my
own. I trust in your Word that never fails. You don't go
back on your promises and you follow it all through to the
end. May my heart take hope in that truth again. When I
look back over my history with you, I can't help but see the
fingerprints of faithfulness written all over it.

What do you know to be lasting and true?

Peace at Every Turn

The Messiah has come to preach this sweet message of peace to you, the ones who were distant, and to those who are near.

EPHESIANS 2:17 TPT

Messiah, you lovingly call us into your kingdom, like an attentive shepherd gathering his sheep. You haven't excluded anyone from your family, and you never will. You don't turn away the beggar or the orphan, but you set them in families and provide for their every need. I have known the comfort of belonging to you, and I have also known the pain of this world. One does not cancel out the other.

You, Lord, are full of peace at every turn. It can't be separated from your nature, and I trust that you will calm every anxiety in my heart with your presence. I need you more than I can say, and I always will. I long for you to restore rest to my soul—would you do it again?

Where do you need peace to meet you today?

Secret Strength

I know what it is to be in need, and I know what it is to have plenty. I have learned the secret of being content in any and every situation, whether well fed or hungry, whether living in plenty or in want. I can do all this through him who gives me strength.

PHILIPPIANS 4:12-13 NIV

God my strength, you see me in my weakness and in my thriving. You don't ever withhold your hand of comfort from me when I need it. You are so much better than the consolation I find in the world. When I am surrounded by community and am drawing strength from them, what a beautiful glimpse it is into the way you work. When I feel isolated, would you surround me with the embrace of your presence that leaves no pain untouched?

Whether I am feeling good about the day or I am just longing for it to be over with, I know that you are the same through it all. You are constant in love and consistent in kindness. May my heart find the strength it needs today to hold onto hope. May I be filled with your peace that brings clarity to every situation. You are the driving force of my life. When I am connected to you, I lack nothing.

*Does your confidence change
based on your circumstances?*

Spirit Satisfaction

The kingdom of God is not eating and drinking, but
righteousness and peace and joy in the Holy Spirit.

ROMANS 14:17 NASB

King of kings, you are higher than any other name. Your
authority is the ultimate, and your power is unmatched
in all the world. Your perspective takes every detail into
account, and you're just and true in all of your decisions.
You don't rule with an iron fist; you lead in mercy and draw
every heart in kindness.

It is easy for me to see where my life is out of whack when
I consider the fruit of your Spirit. Where there is fear,
your love comes rushing in. Where I am trying to control
different aspects and outcomes, there is peace in letting
go. Where there is pain that is not subsiding, there is
comfort in your presence and healing in your words. Meet
me with the power of your life in mine and align my life to
your kingdom values.

*Where do you see evidence of the fruit of the Spirit
in your life?*

Filled with Kindness

The LORD is righteous in everything he does;
he is filled with kindness.

PSALM 145:17 NLT

Lord, when I am tempted to focus on my troubles, would you shift my awareness to see where your kindness is present in my life? Your love never leaves me; your Word is clear about that. Your peace is not some flimsy gift that can be easily broken. Your power is beyond the most influential leaders on the earth. No one can talk you out of your mercy, and what you set in motion cannot be deterred.

Fill my heart with your love again, Lord. I rely on your character to lead me through every dark night of the soul as well the bright, sunny days of my joy. I know that these circumstances won't last, and I won't be in the depths of mourning forever. Lift me up when I can't keep going on my own. In your kindness, I find the comfort I need for every moment.

Where do you see God's kindness right now?

Look No Further

Since we have been justified by faith, we have peace
with God through our Lord Jesus Christ.

ROMANS 5:1 ESV

God, you are the sustainer of my hope and the peace that
calms every doubt and fear. When my heart wavers in
faith, struggling to hold onto any semblance of hopeful
expectation, you steady me with your consistent grace.
You hold the keys to life and the solutions to every problem
I encounter. Why would I look for answers anywhere else?

Keep me secure in your perfect love, calming every anxiety
and quieting the distracting noise of the world. You are the
one who holds me when everything is falling apart. You do
not leave me to pick up the pieces of my life on my own;
you are a masterful restorer, and I rely on you to make
something beautiful out of the disorder around me. Don't
let me down, Lord. You are my peace and the source of
deep, lasting joy for my soul.

Where do you look for peace?

Unchanging One

Answer me, O LORD, for your steadfast love is good;
according to your abundant mercy, turn to me.

PSALM 69:16 NRSV

Merciful One, I turn to you again today. It doesn't matter how many times I get distracted from your goodness, you remain constant in your pursuit and steady in your love. You are so good; thank you for not changing with the times. You always offer fresh perspective, and you are always doing something new. You haven't grown stale; you are not like stagnant waters that need to be purified. You are the pure and living waters that my soul longs to be refreshed by, and that will never change.

Answer me again, Lord. I come to you with every question, every need, and all my longings and hopes. You never disappoint; you always show up and follow through. Why does my heart so often wonder whether you will do it, when you have been nothing but faithful? Even in what seemed like a let-down, you wove something more intricate and beautiful than I could have anticipated. You never miss a detail. May my heart come alive in hope and courage again today.

Have you asked God for his perspective on your past?

Covered by Covenant

I know that you will welcome me into your house,
for I am covered by your covenant of mercy and love.
So I come to your sanctuary with deepest awe
to bow in worship and adore you.

PSALM 5:7 TPT

Good Father, you have welcomed me with open arms into your home and family. I take a moment to let that truth soak into my consciousness. You have brought me into your kingdom with the embrace of a Father, and you call me your own. Your will and your promises will come to pass; they are not dependent on me. Partnership with you is a privilege, and I am undone by the thought of it.

I am connected to the living water of your presence. I am bound to your goodness and mercy. What you give, no one can take away. I cannot be kidnapped from your house, and no one can change the name that you have given me. You have sealed me with your love, and nothing can undo it. Thank you for your faithful love that will never let me go.

When was the last time you considered that God's view of you is the one that matters the most?

Priceless Treasure

How priceless is your unfailing love, O God!
People take refuge in the shadow of your wings.
They feast on the abundance of your house;
you give them drink from your river of delights.
For with you is the fountain of life;
in your light we see light.

PSALM 36:7-9 NIV

Great God, you are the bright and morning star. Your love is a fire that continually burns bright, bringing light to everything. In your unfailing love, I am seen and known. Nothing is left untouched by the light of your compassion, and your mercy has not excluded a living thing. You are the safe place I run to in my uncertainty and trouble. In pain, I am comforted by your healing presence.

Why would I look for satisfaction in any temporary and flawed thing when I have access to the source of goodness itself? Your love is worth more than diamonds, and your kindness is purer than refined gold. I run into your heart of affection today; close in around me with your peace that brings rest to my soul. I will drink your presence in; let me taste your goodness even now.

What is your heart longing for today?

Everything Is Covered

They shall neither hunger nor thirst,
Neither heat nor sun shall strike them;
For He who has mercy on them will lead them,
Even by the springs of water He will guide them.

ISAIAH 49:10 NKJV

God, you are my strong shelter and my covering shield. You keep me secure in the center of your love in every moment. I am never outside of your watchful care. May my heart take courage in that realization and reality again today. Lead me in your love to quiet waters where my soul can drink of your waters that restore my strength. I don't need to worry about your provision when I am hand-in-hand with the Creator of everything. You guide me into peace and give me the rest I need.

Would you permeate my mind with the wisdom of your insight? You always bring clarity and focus when my soul is quieted by your love. I may not know the specifics of every step or turn, but you give me enough for right now. You show me the next best thing I can do, and as I follow through, you continue to lead and guide every single step of the way. May my heart continue to trust you.

Have you been waiting for a blueprint to act,
or can you take a small step in the right direction today?

Refreshed

He saved us, not on the basis of deeds which we have
done in righteousness, but according to His mercy,
by the washing of regeneration and renewing
by the Holy Spirit.

TITUS 3:5 NASB

Savior, I am grateful for the reminder of the reality that my
rescue is not dependent on my own goodness. You act in
mercy because you are merciful. Your motives are pure and
you always keep your Word. Where I have been tempted
to question your goodness because of the lack of my own,
I ask for your higher perspective to see how your perfect
love covers everything. All my failure, my doubts, and my
fears are completely taken care of with the covering of
your mercy.

Holy Spirit, wash over the screen of my mind and bring
life to my thoughts. Bring the clarity of your unhindered
perception that separates lies from the truth. I trust that
you will continue to make me new; you will continue to
renew my life. As long as I draw breath, there is hope. You
are my living hope.

Will you let the Holy Spirit renew your mind today?

Watched Over

The LORD keeps you from all harm
and watches over your life.
The LORD keeps watch over you as you come and go,
both now and forever.

PSALM 121:7-8 NLT

Lord, you are the keeper of my soul and you watch over every detail of my life. Nothing escapes your notice! I take comfort in the thought of your tender care of me. As I walk through cycles of sorrow as I grieve, I know that you are with me. You are the one who holds me together when otherwise I would come apart. Your presence sustains me. You are my resilience and strength.

Don't ever let me go, God. I know you won't but reassure me with your powerful presence as a seal and a promise. Keep me from harmful traps. May my heart stay entwined with yours with the thread of your strong love. You are so much better than anyone I've ever known. I'm so grateful for you.

Does your heart know the confident care of your Maker?

I Look to You

To you I lift up my eyes,
O you who are enthroned in the heavens!

PSALM 123:1 NRSV

Mighty God, I lift my eyes to you today. I offer you my attention, and I lay out my heart before you. I trust your kind character to meet, guide, and teach me with your unmatched wisdom. When I am overwhelmed by the craziness of life and the inescapable pain that comes with it, may I build the habit of lifting my gaze to you. You are enthroned in the heavens—you are high above every living thing—yet you are intricately involved in the workings of my life.

I am so thankful that there is not a moment where you are unengaged in my life. I don't need to tell you what I'm going through because you're with me in it. Even in the unexplainable emotions of my soul and the confusion of my heart, you see it clearly and know exactly what I need. I trust you, Lord, to do what only you can. As I continually lift my eyes to you throughout my day, may my heart also be lifted in hope.

When you are overwhelmed with the details of your life, do you take time to look to God?

Focused Attention

We don't focus our attention on what is seen but on
what is unseen. For what is seen is temporary, but the
unseen realm is eternal.

2 CORINTHIANS 4:18 TPT

Eternal One, you are outside the boundaries of time; there
is no beginning or end to you. When I get caught up in
the nitty-gritty of my life and feel like there is no end to
the problems that arise, please redirect my viewpoint.
I want to see from your perspective, where the details
come together in a grandiose puzzle. Help me to trust
your leadership when I cannot see how things will work
together for my good.

Spirit of God, infuse me with your love that sets my heart
on the calm course of trusting you. When faith feels like it
goes against everything in my present reality, empower my
heart to choose to look at your track record of faithfulness.
Even when I cannot see it in the moment, I know that you
are loyal to every promise you make. May the eyes of my
heart be set on you, not on the minutiae of my life.

What have you been giving your attention to lately?

Keep Going

I have fought the good fight,
I have finished the race,
I have kept the faith.

2 TIMOTHY 4:7 NCV

Faithful God, when my heart is weak and I am tempted to throw my hands up in surrender to the overwhelming aspects of life, strengthen me with your love. There are many days when I can only get through and count surviving as a win. When those days slide into weeks, the heaviness of sadness is my companion. You walk with me through it. You are the lifter of my burdens.

Let my soul find rest in you today as I keep going. I haven't given up yet; when I feel like I have nothing good left to look forward to, would you fill me with your presence that breathes hope into my heart? I can't pull myself out of this. Your love covers and surrounds me. Let it be the incubator that revives me to a healthy place once again. In the meantime, I will rest in your presence.

What does it mean to you to persevere?

Choose Forgiveness

Be kind to each other, tenderhearted, forgiving one
another, just as God through Christ has forgiven you.

EPHESIANS 4:32 NLT

Jesus, you are the one I look to for how to live. Your life is a
beautiful example of humble power. You offered forgiveness
and understanding to those who did not deserve it, and
also to those who others would withhold it from. You
exemplified kindness and inclusion. Let my life be one that
glorifies you as I walk through suffering and pain.

Sorrow is not a stranger to you; you know the weight of
grief and pain well. When I feel like I am alone in my grief,
remind me again of your acquaintance with sadness.
Comfort me with the nearness of your presence. When I
want to hold onto grudges and keep people at a distance
with judgment, give me the lens of compassion to see
others the way you approach me. Help me to not be so
consumed with my own pain that I overlook the pain
of others. As I am comforted, let me comfort. As I am
forgiven, let me also forgive.

When your pain is isolating, what helps you invite others in?

A Better Way

The word of the LORD is upright,
and all his work is done in faithfulness.

PSALM 33:4 ESV

Lord, I want to walk in your perfect way of love. Everything you do is marked by your faithfulness. I trust that even when I cannot understand how you will work a situation out for my good, you will not fail to weave your goodness into it. Help me to rest in your love when my heart is tempted to jump ahead with worry. As I take a few moments to reorient my attention on you, fill me with your peace that slows down my thoughts and brings clarity.

When my heart is wanting to trust but is caught up in the chaos of unexpected triggers, would you come close with your peace and calm anxiety? I need you more than I can articulate, God. I know that you never give up; strengthen my heart to trust that where I am is where you are working right now.

What can you release to God today?

God's Goodness

Do you despise the riches of His goodness, forbearance,
and longsuffering, not knowing that the goodness of
God leads you to repentance?

ROMANS 2:4 NKJV

Good God, you are perfect in all of your ways. Where
there is disappointment in this life, there is a lack of
understanding of how great you truly are. It's not that
I need to convince myself that you are better than my
experience; I don't need to force my mind into submission
under the guise of self-control. It is your love that changes
everything. I can logically understand something, but until I
emotionally experience it, it is one-dimensional.

Holy Spirit, guide me in your goodness today. Flood my
senses with your kindness, filling every cell and pore. I'm
done with my striving; lead me in love. Thank you for
mercy that meets me right where I am in every moment. I
don't have to clean myself up in order to be accepted by
you; I already am, just as I am.

Which is the better motivator in your life—love or shame?

Compassion for All

> "I will have mercy on whom I have mercy, and I will have compassion on whom I have compassion."
>
> ROMANS 9:15 NRSV

God over all, you are endlessly compassionate to your children. I don't understand how you never tire of showing your love. I don't get how you can be so patient with me when I regularly question your goodness—even after I have experienced it. And yet, here we are. You have not changed your mind about me, and I will not disqualify myself from being loved by you. You are so much kinder than I could ever be, and I'm so thankful for your mercy.

Thank you for goodness that knows no end. I will take a moment and let this truth sink in. There is no limit to your love, no cap to your forgiveness. I won't keep myself from you today. Love me to life again, Lord. There is no other who can make my soul come alive like you. I feel like I'm experiencing everything for the first time when you breathe your compassion into my heart and mind. I see you, Lord, and I ask for more!

Have you talked yourself out of receiving God's love because of your own failings?

June

"Whatever you ask in prayer, believe that you have received it, and it will be yours."

MARK 11:24 ESV

Strength for Today

Be strong and courageous. Do not be afraid or terrified
because of them, for the Lord your God goes with you;
he will never leave you nor forsake you.

DEUTERONOMY 31:6 NIV

Lord my God, I have everything I need with you by my side.
What a wonderful reality that your presence goes with me
wherever I am. Your reminder to be strong and courageous
helps me to stand strong in the resolve of your unfailing
love. If you are with me, I lack nothing. When my heart
starts to quiver with worry, would you steady me with your
perfect peace? As long as you are my constant companion,
I can walk through anything.

Today, Holy Spirit, fill me with courage to take a step
forward in you, even in the face of fear. With you by my
side, I am taken care of in every season and situation. Take
me by the hand and lead me into your goodness; you are
present in mercy and persistent in peace. I will trust you!

In what area has fear kept you stuck?

Alive in Christ

God, being rich in mercy, because of His great love with which He loved us, even when we were dead in our transgressions, made us alive together with Christ (by grace you have been saved).

EPHESIANS 2:4-5 NASB

Merciful God, every new day I am met by your compassion. I am made complete in your love; you renew me over and over again. Because of your great love, every moment is a new opportunity to be washed clean and refreshed in your presence. I won't take that for granted today but come running into your arms of grace again. Thank you for renewal, Jesus. Your life in mine is what gives me hope for tomorrow and strength for today.

Where there is sadness in my heart, bring joy. Where there is discouragement, breathe hope. Where there is confusion, settle peace over my mind. You are so much better than the treasure I find on earth that eventually would be lost or destroyed. You never diminish in beauty or wonder. Flood my heart again with the revelation of your immense goodness!

Do you see evidence of Jesus' life in your own?

Tender Mercy

His unforgettable works of surpassing wonder
reveal his grace and tender mercy.

PSALM 111:4 TPT

Wonderful Counselor, you are always moving in mercy.
You never stop working for our good, and you don't grow
weary in revealing your grace to all who look to you. I lift
my eyes to you again today, Lord, and I long for a new
perspective of your hand on my life. I know you haven't
given up on me even when I feel completely defeated by
the world and its ways.

Work in wonder in my life, Lord. Let me see your goodness
in unmistakable ways. Where I see gaping holes of lack in
my life, and messes of chaos that seem more jumbled than a
knotted ball of twinkle lights, fill in the gaps and smooth out
the kinks with your grace. Here's my life, Lord. Don't leave a
corner of it untouched by your overwhelming kindness.

*Where do you see a need for God's mercy
to bring calm to your life?*

What Matters Most

Three things will last forever—
faith, hope, and love—
and the greatest of these is love.

1 Corinthians 13:13

Compassionate One, I raise my awareness above the fray of my life today and turn my attention to you, my liberator. Though this life is but a breath—it goes so quickly—you have neither beginning nor end. You are eternal, and your character is never-ending. When despair threatens to sink my heart, you remind me that hope is everlasting. Fill me with confident expectation of your goodness that is always near. When disappointment leads to doubt that endangers the faith I have clung to, give me fresh eyes to see that you are not done with me yet.

Lord, when my heart feels depleted by all that is required of me by family, friends, and the world in general, wash over me with your love that covers everything. Fill me to overflowing, that what I give would be out of abundance and not the dregs of my soul. Let your lasting love be my fuel forever.

*Where you see gaping needs, will you invite God
to fill you afresh today?*

Coming Back Home

Let the wicked forsake their way,
and the unrighteous their thoughts;
let them return to the LORD,
that he may have mercy on them,
and to our God, for he will abundantly pardon.

ISAIAH 55:7 NRSV

Righteous One, you are full of unending mercy to all who come to you. I will not turn away from you today or even stay in the same space I have been. I focus my heart and my attention on you; you are my home, and in you I find everything I long for fulfilled. You have been with me through my darkest days and in my most joyful moments. You have been consistent through them all.

I return to you today, knowing that you are so much better than anything I'll find outside of your love. You cover me with your kindness and my heart is filled with gratitude. I cannot fully comprehend your affection or understand your unwavering grace that is continually poured out from your heart of love. All I can say today is thank you. Thank you, Father.

What does home feel like to you?

Holy Help

The LORD will fight for you,
and you shall hold your peace.

EXODUS 14:14 NKJV

Just God, you are always quick to rise in my defense, fighting the battles that I cannot. Do it again, Lord—fight for me. I have no strength or strategy of my own; I have exhausted my resources. But you are full of unending kindness toward your children; you are full of wisdom and strength in every circumstance. May my heart be steadied with your perfect peace. Let my mind know the clarity of your perspective in place of the confusion of my limited view.

Lord, look at my life and see where I need your intervention. Even when I don't know how to ask for help, would you intervene in your power and love? You are better than I am, and so much more reliable than even the most faithful heart. I know that you won't fail me; strengthen my heart in your love again today.

*How has God helped you when you had
no hope of relief otherwise?*

Heard

Hear the voice of my pleas for mercy,
when I cry to you for help,
when I lift up my hands toward
your most holy sanctuary.

PSALM 28:2 ESV

Ever-present God, what a relief it is to my heart that you are always near. You always hear me; whether I lift up a shout to you or simply a whisper, you listen closely. You don't miss a beat of my heart, and you certainly don't leave me on my own to fight battles that I am ill-equipped to fight. You are my help in times of trouble. You are my saving grace when I would otherwise be swallowed up in despair.

Come again, Lord. Don't dismiss the cries of my heart or delay your response. As I look through your Word, I see that you faithfully come through. I need to know your persistent presence in ways I haven't before. I have tasted and seen the goodness of your life in mine, but those feel like distant memories today. Do a new thing, Lord, and do it today. Show your faithfulness again.

What do you need from God today?

Shining Star

Do everything without grumbling or arguing, so that you may become blameless and pure, "children of God without fault in a warped and crooked generation." Then you will shine among them like stars in the sky as you hold firmly to the word of life.

PHILIPPIANS 2:14-16 NIV

Father, you are the source of anything good in my life. You are the source of all light and love. You burn like the sun, giving off heat and causing life to grow. I am like a star, reflecting your light in the world. Take me out of the shadow that has fallen over my life. I need you, God, more than I could ever say.

As I walk the road of life with you, lead me into your glorious light. Even when I walk through dark valleys, I know that you are with me. The darkness will not overtake me because you are lighting the path before me even if it's just a step at a time. You hold me close and I am comforted by your nearness. Let my life always reflect yours; you are my covering.

How have your words reflected the attitude of your heart lately?

Endless Kindness

May the LORD show you his kindness
and have mercy on you.

NUMBERS 6:25 NCV

Lord, you are endlessly compassionate and kind. Why would I stay away when in you is the comfort I long for? You care for me perfectly. You don't apply a one-size-fits-all approach to your children; you know exactly how to communicate your goodness in my life in a way that communicates the depths of your affection for me. Reveal your mercy to me in a personal way again today.

You are familiar with the gait of my stride, the way my eyebrows bend when I'm deep in thought, and every mark on my body. You are acutely aware of the rise and fall of my chest when I breathe, and the places my mind goes when it wanders. Just as you know me, I want to know you. Show yourself to me in a new way; I long to know you more. Only you can satisfy my soul!

How has God met you in the details of your life before?

Made Complete

Finally, brethren, rejoice, be made complete,
be comforted, be like-minded, live in peace;
and the God of love and peace will be with you.

2 CORINTHIANS 13:11 NASB

God of love, you offer the clarity of peace in every situation. There isn't a moment when your love leaves. Saturate me with your present affection even now. May my heart experience the joy of being fully known by you; let my soul find strength in knowing you in your endless goodness. You never change and you never will—what a wonder!

When I don't know what to do, I will look to you. When I don't know where to turn, I will turn to you. When I'm at a loss for how to continue, I will follow you. You never fail to lead in love or guide in perfect wisdom. With my life joined to yours, I will be led into the fullness of your kingdom's ways and purposes. Even today, I will live like Jesus did—in love, in reliance on the Father's direction, and in trust of his ultimate plan.

How can you align your life in love today?

No More Walls

He himself is our peace, who has made us both one and has broken down in his flesh the dividing wall of hostility.

EPHESIANS 2:14 ESV

Peace giver, I look to you to make what is off kilter in my life right in you. Your perspective is perfect and you always have a way out of the messes of life. You have removed every obstacle there was in being one with you. There is no distance that is not closed by one step on your part. Though, at times, I have felt like there is a wall of pain and shame that hides me from you, I know that you have torn down everything that would keep me from your love. If anything remains, it is love.

Wash over my mind with your mercy today and let me sense you with me right here and now. Cause hope to spring up as you saturate my heart in your comforting presence. There is no one like you, who fights for me and keeps pursuing me even in my wandering. Let today be a day of unmistakable restoration.

Is there anything that feels like it has put distance between you and God?

Overflowing Affection

Look at how much encouragement you've found in your relationship with the Anointed One! You are filled to overflowing with his comforting love. You have experienced a deepening friendship with the Holy Spirit and have felt his tender affection and mercy.

PHILIPPIANS 2:1 TPT

Holy Spirit, you are the best gift I've ever known. You consistently move in power in my life, covering every area with the mercy of God. Your presence is life to me; you breathe peace, and my heart is calmed. You saturate me with the oil of your love, and it is sweet and nourishing to my soul. You always give in abundance, filling to overflowing, so I have something to offer as well.

May today be full of deepening friendship with you. You walk with me, and I with you, into every situation and circumstance. You are closer than my skin, and you constantly impart strength when I have none. May my awareness of you be unquestionable as I go about my routine. You are a constant companion, a wise counselor, and the closest comfort I've ever known. Thank you for being with me in every moment.

Are you aware of God's constant presence in your life?

Greater Reality

Great is your mercy, O Lord;
give me life according to your justice.

Psalm 119:156 NRSV

Lord, I know that your ways are higher than mine and your thoughts see the bigger picture while still accounting for every detail. You are full of wisdom for every problem in life, and you have the keys to overcoming every obstacle. I rely on you, not on my own strength, as I face another day. I submit my mind to you, asking that you would wash over it with your peace that makes even the difficult seem simple.

You are fair and righteous in all your decisions. You don't mow over some in favor of lifting up others; you offer the same portion of love to all, which is endless. I don't want to rely on my own logic or understanding; I've tried that in the past, and it only gets me so far. You are better, and so are your ways. I align my heart with yours; guide me in your truth.

Are you being led by love in every area of your life?

Victory

Every child of God defeats this evil world, and we achieve this victory through our faith.

1 John 5:4 NLT

Father, you are perfect in the way you parent. Your intentions are good, and your motives are pure. You teach your children how to live with the fullness of love as their fuel. I am yours, and I belong to you. You have promised that I will not be taken down by the world, but that I will overcome it with faith. Teach me how to do this. I know that you are patient in direction and will lift me up every time I try and then fail.

Thank you for grace that covers my weakness and joy that assures me that I am learning to become more like you even when I don't get it right. You don't expect perfection from me; you just want my willingness. Give me perseverance to keep going and trying again. Fill me with your love at every moment, so shame would have no place in my heart. Let your affection constantly warm me like the sun on my skin, soaking in deep and bringing peace and joy.

As a child of God, what does victory look like in your life?

He Is Coming

"I will make all my goodness pass before you and will proclaim before you my name 'The Lord.' And I will be gracious to whom I will be gracious, and will show mercy on whom I will show mercy."

EXODUS 33:19 ESV

Great God, I long for your goodness to pass before me just like it did with Moses. I have known of you, and I have surely seen evidence of your loving hand on my life, but I want more. I am not satisfied with yesterday's portion; I need a fresh revelation of your presence in my life. I want to see you in a new way!

In your kindness, make yourself known to me in an undeniable way. I have eyes; let them see you. I have ears; let them hear you. I know that you are the one who feeds the hunger in my heart—only you can quench the thirst of my soul. Do it, Lord, in a new way. You don't grow weary in love, so meet me with the abundance of your affection today. Here I am; connect with me.

Do you hesitate to ask God for more?

A Thousand Generations

Know that the LORD your God, He is God, the faithful God who keeps covenant and mercy for a thousand generations with those who love Him and keep His commandments.

DEUTERONOMY 7:9 NKJV

Faithful One, you are constant throughout the ages. What you have spoken, you will cause to pass, and what you have promised will be fulfilled. Your covenant is sealed by your loyal character that does not deceive. You are consistent in mercy and full of kindness toward all who come to you. As I look over history, may I see the thread of your mercy woven through the ages. As I consider the works of your hands, may my heart be encouraged in your power at work in the present.

You will not forsake your people or abandon those who seek you. You are a constant help and presence in time of trouble. There isn't a moment where you leave me to rely on my own strength; with my life tethered to yours, I find that your leadership is kind and you won't ever let me go. Encourage my heart in your love again today!

Can you see the evidence of
God's faithfulness around you?

So Good

LORD, answer me because your love is so good.
Because of your great kindness, turn to me.

PSALM 69:16 NCV

Lord, when my heart is discouraged, meet me with the
kindness of your presence. Radiate your light of love on my
life that I may see where you are already at work. Remind
me of your goodness that has been with me. I trust that
you are still better than I know. You are so far beyond my
understanding; I can only imagine the length of your love—
and yet the reality of it is incomprehensible.

When I am afraid, I turn to you. Lord, I can't hide the qualms
of my heart; sadness has opened the door to questions that
had previously been untapped. But you, God, aren't worried
about my misgivings. You don't change based on my idea
of you. In your love, reveal yourself to me. Let me see your
goodness as plain as day. I rely on you, God. Answer me
and turn to me in your mercy again today.

When was the last time you tasted
the goodness of God's love?

Yes You Are

Once you were not a people, but now you are God's
people; once you had not received mercy,
but now you have received mercy.

1 PETER 2:10 ESV

Father, I come to you as a child today, knowing I am always
welcome in your presence. Where I have been hanging
back in hesitation, I let down every hindrance and come
running to you. I know you won't disappoint me; you are
the most transparent heart I have ever known. Your love is
strong enough to cover every fear, every doubt, and every
failure I could ever make. Your mercy is endless—it can't
ever be tapped.

Where I have disqualified myself because of my own lack
of faith or the ability to measure up, you assure me that
your love is the measure, not my own. You more than cover
every lack I have. I won't exclude myself as your child
because of my weakness; you certainly don't. Today, I am
reminded that your perfect love is the sea that washes my
sin away. Your compassion is greater than my misgivings.

*What criteria have you placed on yourself
as God's child that he never did?*

Led by Truth

Guide me in your truth and teach me,
for you are God my Savior,
and my hope is in you all day long.

PSALM 25:5 NIV

Savior, you are the leader of my life. In you I find the freedom for which my heart so desperately longs. You guide me into truth as I follow you on your pathway of peace. You are my help when I am lost, my confidence when I am undone, and my covering when I am vulnerable. Let my heart find its rest in you again today as you fight for me.

Let your wisdom be my advisor as I venture in this life. I don't lean on my own understanding today; I yield my ways to yours, knowing that you always see the bigger picture. Where I am likely to fail, even there, your wisdom leads me through. I will keep pressing on and pressing into you as I go about my day. You are my holy help; may my heart take courage in the knowledge that you are with me.

Do you trust God to guide you through uncertainty?

Hemmed In

The LORD is near to all who call on him,
yes, to all who call on him in truth.

PSALM 145:18 NLT

Lord, when my heart trembles at the start of a new day,
and my mind races with the uncertainties of ambiguous
outcomes, calm me with the peace of your presence. I call on
you again today. You have been faithful to answer, and I trust
that you will draw near again in your tangible love. Quiet my
mind with the clarity of your wisdom and set my heart at rest
in the safety of your tender care. You won't feed me to the
wolves or abandon me to fight my own battles.

Your power is at work within my life even now; I know it.
Give me eyes to see what you're doing and confidence
to trust that you won't stop working for my good. I don't
need riches or glory; I just want the peace that you offer.
Bring freedom to my heart as I lean into your mercy again
today. Let faith conquer fear as your grace empowers my
heart to trust.

How do you sense God's nearness in your life?

Miracles of Mercy

Lift your hands and give thanks to God
for his marvelous kindness
and for his miracles of mercy for those he loves!

PSALM 107:8 TPT

Merciful Father, you are the giver of all good gifts. When my heart is hesitant to ask you for what it truly needs, may I have the courage to use my voice and the favor I have as your child. You are a good and generous parent; why would I hold myself back from you when you never turn me away? Today, with a breath of thanks on my lips, I will name all that has been stagnant or stirring within me. You are gracious. Let our interaction today be a testament to that.

Your miracles of mercy are already in my life; your marvelous kindness is beyond any I have encountered on this earth. Here I am with my full heart overflowing; let this exchange between full hearts be more than I could hope for today. Astound me with your unfailing love yet again, Lord!

Will you bring God all that is in your heart today?

God's Terms

It depends not on human will or exertion,
but on God, who has mercy.

ROMANS 9:16 ESV

God, as I lay down my worries before you today, may my heart find rest in your capable hands. There is always more to do, checklists to be conquered, and people to be pacified. I don't have the capacity to keep everything straight, let alone keep people happy. I am grateful for the reminder today in your Word that your mercy works more efficiently than my own efforts. As I lean back into your love right now, I will allow the anxious thoughts to be collected by you. Make my mind peaceful in your presence.

I join my hand to yours, and my heart to yours again and trust you to do a better job than I can with the details of my life. There is only so much I can do in a day, but your power is infinite. I'm so grateful for your goodness that is lining my life. Keep me at rest in you as I continually hand over what isn't mine to do and help me see that from a place of rest my productivity actually grows. Thank you.

What have you been trying to keep track of that isn't yours to do?

Give Thanks

Oh, give thanks to the LORD, for He is good!
For His mercy endures forever.

1 CHRONICLES 16:34 NKJV

Wonderful God, let the first words off my lips right now be those of thanks. What an amazing God you are, that you always meet me with your mercy and your goodness is your greeting. I want to be like you, dripping with life and love to all those around me. Even so, I will not forget your goodness in the hard and dry times. When I am running low, your compassion is always rushing to meet me. When I have nothing to offer others because of the sorrow that weighs heavy on my soul, you say that I am not what I do—not even what I do for you. What acceptance—what love!

I am so grateful to be loved by a gracious and wonderful Father who never abandons me. You are always readily available and quick to reveal your presence in the nitty-gritty. I rely on you more than I could ever clue into; in all things, may my heart be quick to give you thanks whether with a whisper, a nod, or a shout.

What can you thank God for today?

Good Gifts

Grace, mercy and peace will be with us, from God the
Father and from Jesus Christ, the Son of the Father,
in truth and love.

2 JOHN 1:3 NASB

Good God, you have all that I need in life. Even when things
are falling apart and I can't see a way out, I know that you
are there and that you will provide for me. I rely on your
mercy in every twist and turn in life. I can't convince myself
to be okay when I'm not, but I know that you are always
abounding in kindness and comfort when I need it. You don't
yell at me to be better or to do more; rather, you surround
me with your affection and calm me with your peace.

I know that if I am not living with your goodness evident
before my eyes, then this is not the end for me. Lead me
into your abundant love, Lord, and meet me with your
mercy even and especially in the midst of suffering. You are
more than enough—more than all I need. When my heart
despairs, hold it tenderly in your hands and breathe your
life over it once again. Give me eyes to see clues of your
goodness in the here and now.

What gifts do you see that God has deposited in your life?

Keep Me Close

I have tried hard to find you—
don't let me wander from your commands.

PSALM 119:10 NLT

Holy Spirit, draw me close to the heart of the Father today.
Let your compassion be the cord that tethers me to you.
I have searched for you; I have tried my best to pick out
your attributes in the line-up of my life. Even so, my worth
is not wrapped up in my part in this—what I do or don't do
for you. You call me child, and you love me just as I am. I
will never be loved more or loved less than I am right now
in this very moment. Your love does not get bigger on my
good days and diminish on my less than stellar ones.

Here you are, in the fullness of your love. And here I am,
open to receive your uninhibited affection. Flood me with
your love right now; in your kindness, reveal your tender
heart once again. Faithfully envelop me like a mother
embraces her child.

*Will you invite God to reveal his affection toward you
in a new way?*

Gracious God

In Your great mercy You did not utterly consume them
nor forsake them;
For You are God, gracious and merciful.

NEHEMIAH 9:31 NKJV

Kind One, you are full of mercy. In my suffering, you do not let me be consumed by the pain. You haven't abandoned me in my messes—not even one. You are the constant one, always emanating compassion. You are kinder than any other; your patience never runs out, and you are not intimidated by any of the misgivings I have about you, the world, or myself.

Meet me with the fullness of your mercy today; remove everything that keeps me from you. Overshadow the shame I feel with your powerful love and affection. Do not leave me to destruction—not even by my own hand. Break me free from the cycles of destruction and set my feet on the solid foundation of your grace. Show me the lengths your love goes to rescue. Let my mind be free of the cluttered chaos of lies, shame, doubt, and rage. You are better. May your peace be my portion now and forever.

*Where you feel at a breaking point,
can you reach out for help?*

Abundance

God is able to bless you abundantly,
so that in all things at all times,
having all that you need,
you will abound in every good work.

2 CORINTHIANS 9:8 NIV

God of abundance, you are as generous in mercy right in this moment as you ever have been. May my heart be encouraged today as I receive your boundless grace that empowers me for everything I face in life. You always provide what I need; where I look at my life and see lack, there is an invitation for your power to be made evident in your provision.

Lord, hear the cries of my heart beyond the obvious needs that are clear in my life. How I long for your love to flow over and through me once again, overtaking every fear that has kept me stuck. You are so much better than my little logic allows for. Your comfort is always with me when I need it; where I have been running on empty, God, would you come and fill me once again with your power and peace that goes far beyond my understanding? I yield my heart, my mind, and my life to you once again trusting in your goodness.

How have you recognized God's provision in your life?

Never Abandoned

I had said in my alarm,
"I am cut off from your sight."
But you heard the voice of my pleas for mercy
when I cried to you for help.

PSALM 31:22 ESV

Faithful One, today I am reminded of your loyal love that never leaves me in my suffering. You do not turn away from me when I spiral in loneliness and despair. You don't try to lecture me out of my sorrow. What a wonderful Father you are, always reaching out in comfort and compassion. You wrap around me with the peace of your presence whenever I need it.

Meet me with your goodness again today, and redirect my point of view, Lord. Let me see from your higher perspective rather than my limited understanding. I know that I see in part, but you see the whole picture from beginning to end—not just in my life. You see the entire trajectory of the world. I won't stop turning to you for help, and I know that you will never turn me away. You don't just tolerate me; you delight in me! What a wonderful reminder.

What would it look like to see your life from God's perspective today?

Resurrection Life

If while we were still enemies, God fully reconciled us to himself through the death of his Son, then something greater than friendship is ours. Now that we are at peace with God, and because we share in his resurrection life, how much more we will be rescued from sin's dominion!

ROMANS 5:10 TPT

Holy One, let every thought that denies your power be brought into alignment with your matchless wonder and worth. You are the miracle maker, the mountain mover, and the God of the impossible. In resurrection life, the power of sin and death was rendered defeated. You made a way where there seemed to be none and at the highest price. Thank you, God, that I am not just a friend of yours—though that would be enough. As a child of the Father of lights, I am a reflection of the same love that risked everything for freedom and unity.

Lord, I invite your power to move in my life in the same way that Jesus was raised to life forever. Bring new life out of the ashes; bring restoration where there is destruction. Redeem that which has been taken from me and breathe hope into the caverns of my heart that await your life-giving light.

Where do you need the power of resurrection life to meet you?

Come Close

Let us then with confidence draw near to the throne of grace, that we may receive mercy and find grace to help in time of need.

HEBREWS 4:16 ESV

Merciful Lord, I come with confidence before your throne of grace today. I won't hold back anything as I approach you. Here's my heart, open wide before you. Here's my life, Lord, I loosen my grip and invite you to do what only you can do and what I could only dream of doing. The seeds of life you sow in me are so much better than my measly attempts at control will ever produce.

You don't miss a beat. It doesn't matter how often or how little I turn my attention to you; your affection for me never wavers. What an amazing, merciful Father you are, that you always welcome me with open arms! I am undone by your loving attention every time I receive it. May my heart be ever attuned to you, and may I find my true identity in the reflection of your affection.

Are you convinced of God's unwavering love for you?

July

He will answer the prayers of the needy;
he will not reject their prayers.

PSALM 102:17 NCV

He Is Better

To the Lord our God belong mercy and forgiveness,
though we have rebelled against Him.

DANIEL 9:9 NKJV

Lord God, you are incredibly patient in your compassion.
You don't rush me to make a decision or even pressure me
to choose you. Your kindness constantly draws me back
to you every time I choose my own way and fail. You do
not disqualify me from being your child when I mess up.
Rather, as a patient and loving Father, you embrace me
with your sympathy and kindly teach me your ways.

I'm so thankful that you are better than my own limited
experience reveals. But I can see your fingerprint of mercy
even in my small life. You have been with me every step of
my life's journey. Continue to lead me in love all the days
of my life and correct my perspective when I lower mine to
the world's skewed view. Open my eyes to see through the
clear lens of your wisdom and let compassion be the fire
that fuels my heart.

Do you relate to God as a patient and loving Father?

Constant Comfort

Your words have comforted those who fell,
and you have strengthened those who could not stand.

JOB 4:4 NCV

Comforter, wrap your arms of love around me again today. Your presence infuses me with peace, and you are the respite my soul longs for. It doesn't matter how short or how long it's been since I rested in your perfect love; you never withhold your tender mercy from me at any moment. May my heart be strengthened in you as you hold me together.

Spirit of God, come close even now. Don't make me beg you for a fresh encounter with your love. I know that's not how you work. You are attentive and kind, and you meet my heart's needs with the provision of your grace. Every time I look to you, you sow seeds of life within me. I know I will see the fruit of your life in mine. May my heart rest in your perfect timing. Keep me steady in your love today and every day.

When words fail, what brings you comfort?

Holy Exchange

"Blessed are the poor in spirit,
for theirs is the kingdom of heaven.
Blessed are those who mourn,
for they will be comforted."

MATTHEW 5:3-4 NIV

King of heaven, you rule over every submitted heart with unconditional love. You are powerful in mercy and tender in kindness. I don't have much to offer you, Lord. You see that clearly, and I know it well. My attempts to love you are flawed but genuine. When pain rips my heart open, I can barely get through the day. Survival mode becomes the default when my grief is great.

I'm thankful that you are not looking for positive people. You are after willing hearts. You more than make up the difference of everything I lack, and I trust that your love is strong enough to get me through the darkest nights of my soul. Be the rock beneath me—my firm foundation. Even when I fall, I will fall on you. I cannot be moved from you.

How is God's tender care of you manifested in your life?

Way of Peace

"Because of the tender mercy of our God,
With which the Sunrise from on high will visit us,
To shine upon those who sit in darkness and the
shadow of death,
To guide our feet into the way of peace."

LUKE 1:78-79 NASB

Merciful God, guide me on your pathway of peace. There's no other road I want to walk. Your love runs deeper, your peace truer, and your mercy greater than any other. You have no counterpart; there is no other like you. You are rich in compassion and generous in kindness. With you as my loving leader, why would I want to go any other way? You bring life out of destruction and beauty out of ashes. That's my God.

Shine on me again today with the light of your love. You bring clarity and calm with you wherever you go. Blow like a summer breeze, refreshing my soul in the rest that you give. I long to be found in you all the days of my life. Let my heart know your steady presence and my mind your clarifying truth. I am yours.

What does peace look like to you?

Drink Deep

"I am the Alpha and the Omega—the Beginning and the End. To all who are thirsty I will give freely from the springs of the water of life."

REVELATION 21:6 NLT

Lord over all, you are both the beginning and the end. Your presence is constant in the day-to-day, and there isn't a moment when you are not with me. You freely give your life to all who ask for it, so here I am asking for more. Your love is like a spring that never runs dry and is full of the purest, clearest, most refreshing water ever tasted.

Let me drink deep of your waters of life again today. Remind me of the purity of what you offer. Jesus, you said that when one drinks of your living waters they will never thirst again. I have tasted and seen your goodness in my life and nothing else satisfies the way you do. You, Lord, are always satisfying in the same measure; you consistently give out of the abundance of your heart. You are my portion today and forever.

What are you thirsty for today?

Marvelous Mercy

Magnify the marvels of your mercy to all who seek you.
Make your Pure One wonderful to me,
like you do for all those who turn aside
to hide themselves in you.

PSALM 17:7 TPT

Pure One, I hide myself in you again today. You see what I'm facing; I am weary of the world and its weight. I can't bear the burdens alone. I believe that you are unchanging and that your character doesn't have a dark side. Your goodness is better than I hope for at every bend in my story. When I look back on this season, I trust that I will see your mercy as evident as the spring flowers in bloom. When I couldn't see beneath the surface of the hard, cold ground, there were seeds and bulbs resting until the conditions were met for blossoming.

You are always at work, Lord; I believe that even when I can't see it. May hope stir in my heart, even the faintest bit, where it has been dormant. You will make all things grow that are meant to because you are the master gardener. I trust your process and timing.

*Do you see evidence of God's mercy
when you look back over hard seasons?*

Ready Relief

Blessed be the God and Father of our Lord Jesus Christ,
the Father of mercies and God of all comfort, who
comforts us in all our affliction so that we will be able to
comfort those who are in any affliction with the comfort
with which we ourselves are comforted by God.

2 CORINTHIANS 1:3-4 NASB

Father of mercy, in my sorrow I let myself come undone
in your presence. I couldn't hold myself together if I tried.
You are patient to sit with me in my discomfort and hold
me close in your compassion. You don't expect me to
process the pain I'm experiencing quickly or move on from
my sadness rooted in loss. You are the closest comfort I've
ever known and relief to my soul.

When you support me with your unfailing affection, the
strength of your love keeps me rooted in who you are and
in who I am in you. As I am loved to life, even in my darkest
moments, I lean into your example of boundless mercy. As I
experience it, so will I be able to offer it. I trust that in your
time, nothing will have been wasted. Use every bit of this
and turn it into beauty beyond my imagining.

What have been the moments of relief within your grief?

Wonderful Wisdom

The wisdom from above is first pure, then peaceable,
gentle, open to reason, full of mercy and good fruits,
impartial and sincere.

JAMES 3:17 ESV

All-knowing God, you see everything through the lens of
love. You see every detail—from the beginning of time
to the end—and you don't miss a moment. Your mercy is
greater than time itself. Your love cannot be bound by any
limits. It is higher than the heavens, deeper than the ocean,
and wider than any human's understanding. You are full of
patience, always willing to lend an ear, and you are readily
available to all who want to know you.

Your sincerity is unmatched; there is no shadow of doubt in
you. You are light and wisdom itself. In you, all living things
find their being. I want to know you more, Lord; I want to
be full of the goodness of your presence. I want to live
according to your wonderful wisdom. Fill my thoughts with
your revelation light and bring understanding to my heart
today. I look to you.

Is your life being led by wisdom?

You See Me

You do see! Indeed you note trouble and grief,
that you may take it into your hands;
the helpless commit themselves to you;
you have been the helper of the orphan.

PSALM 10:14 NRSV

Good Father, I fall into your arms of grace again today. On the days I struggle to get out of bed, you sit with me in my pain. You wrap your comfort around me like a blanket. I am tucked tightly into your love. When all I can do is breathe in and out and repeat that action over and over again, I will not despair in my weakness. I choose to rest here in your loving arms.

Lord, let my heart be saturated with your compassion as you seep into every crack and wound. You are healing salve to my soul. Instead of trying to simply survive the day, I give you the reins and rest in your leadership. You know exactly what I need today, and I trust you to provide it.

Will you let go of your ideas of what life should look like and let God be with you in what it is right now?

It Is Time

Sow for yourselves righteousness;
Reap in mercy;
Break up your fallow ground,
For it is time to seek the Lord,
Till He comes and rains righteousness on you.

HOSEA 10:12 NKJV

Lord, you are the source of my strength and every provision I'll ever need. I set my heart and intentions on you again today. You see how I've struggled to even just get through some days. You've seen me at my lowest point, and I know that you do not judge my weakness. Yet, even in my frailty, I am not left on my own. I lean on your unfailing love; it is the river that moves me through life.

Today, when I am tempted to give into fear and stay stuck in unhelpful routines, I will direct my attention to you and let your comfort be the strength I need to make better choices. Your grace empowers me to choose you and your ways over my own every time. And when I don't, there is your mercy meeting me again. Let my life reflect your kind nature.

*Have you been letting fear keep you stuck
in destructive cycles?*

No Fear

Even though I walk through the darkest valley,
I will fear no evil, for you are with me;
your rod and your staff, they comfort me.

PSALM 23:4 NIV

Good Shepherd, you are such a wise and loving leader. Your compassion gently corrects me when I start to wander. Your mercy brings me back into safe pastures when I have gone off into enemy territory. You are endlessly kind and patient with me. Of that, I'm grateful. I never need to fear the darkness when I know that you are my constant companion and guide.

In your goodness, reveal yourself to me again today. I long to know you more; I've tasted and seen your mercy in my life. I'm hungry for your presence; I'm thirsty for your love. Saturate me with the oil of your presence and satisfy the longings of my heart today. In you is all I'm searching for; even when I don't feel that in my heart, I know it is true. Reveal yourself in a new way!

What hesitation is in your heart toward God?

He Still Heals

"I have seen what they have done,
but I will heal them.
I will guide them and comfort them
and those who felt sad for them.
They will all praise me."

ISAIAH 57:18 NCV

Perfect One, here I am again before your throne of grace. It doesn't matter the state of my life or heart, you accept me as lovingly as you do when I'm at my most devoted simply because I am your child. You don't ever turn me away. Thank you for your kindness that always covers my weakness. Your perfect nature is the standard of your love, not my response to it. Even in my rebellion, your mercy is strong enough to lead me into freedom.

Take notice of the areas of my life that are out of alignment with your goodness and bring them into orientation with your perfect love. Heal my body, my mind, and my heart; I know that you don't ever stop offering restoration and renewal. May my heart find wholeness in you—flood my body with your peace that is beyond logic. You are my King, and I belong to you.

In what areas of your life do you need healing?

My Life's Song

My loving God, the harp in my heart will praise you.
Your faithful heart toward us
will be the theme of my song.
Melodies and music will rise to you,
the Holy One of Israel.

PSALM 71:22 TPT

Holy One, when I think about your faithfulness, I can't help but find my heart hoping once again. When I'm all out of my own resources of faith, help me to remember to look at what you have done and are doing in your people around me. Even when I walk through a dark desert, refresh me with springs of your living water. I know the harsh reality of my circumstances will not always look this way. But you are with me through it all.

Lord, encourage my heart in you again today. Your loyal love never lets go of your children. I have to believe that when I look back on this time of my life I will see your goodness even here. You don't let anything go to waste; you will restore everything. Even now, let a melody of gratefulness mixed with hope fill my heart.

When you look back over your life, where do you see the thread of God's faithfulness?

Joyful Freedom

I prayed to the Lord, and he answered me.
He freed me from all my fears.
Those who look to him for help will be radiant with joy.

PSALM 34:4-5 NLT

Great God, you are my liberator; you lead me into freedom.
When I am afraid, and I feel anxiety's effects flooding my
nervous system, breathe your peace into my body. As I
focus my attention on your presence in my own breath,
calm the response of my brain to the fear that threatens
my ability to engage in this present moment. Lord, you
know exactly what I need precisely when I need it. Don't
overlook my desperation.

Set me free from the cycles that bring me to my knees
and set me on your path of peace. It does not lead me in
endless circles, but it brings me higher as I walk with you
in love. Bring the liberation I so desperately need. As I
look to you, may my face be radiant with the light of your
presence that continually shines on me. You are so near
and so good.

*What fear is keeping you from experiencing
freedom and joy?*

At All Times

May the Lord of peace himself give you peace at all
times and in every way. The Lord be with all of you.

2 THESSALONIANS 3:16 NIV

Mighty God, you are full of power and the most profound
peace I have ever known. Be my constant source of calm
in the chaos of this life. In the dips of grief that feel like
caverns of deep darkness, be my very present peace that
anchors me. In the highs of good days and what looks like
full functioning, be the joy found in the gratefulness of
my heart. There is not one moment where your peace is
absent. It is felt in your very presence.

Be with me today right where I am. You are the helper I
need when I have no clue where to turn or what to do. You
are the confidant I bare my soul to when there is no one
else around. May you be the first one I check in with in the
morning and the last one I speak to when I lay my head
down to sleep. Your constant presence is my strength; I am
so grateful that I am never ever alone.

*How often do you think about
the reality that God is with you?*

My Defense

I will sing of Your power;
Yes, I will sing aloud of Your mercy in the morning;
For You have been my defense
And refuge in the day of my trouble.

PSALM 59:16 NKJV

Defender, I run into the safety of your shelter. Your presence is a shield around me; I don't need to plead my own case when you are fighting for me. Give my heart peace as I rest in you. Calm my racing thoughts as I give over control of my circumstances to you again. I know that you are endless in wisdom and you never wonder what to do. As I choose to trust you, may my heart follow suit and find respite in your tender care.

When I am tempted to take up my own cause, calm my worries with your reassuring words of wisdom. Give me a glimpse of your broad perspective when I get too caught up in the details of my life. You never withhold wisdom from anyone who is searching for it; I won't be disappointed in how you handle any situation as I allow myself to be led by your love. I yield myself to your mercy.

What areas of your life have you been trying to control to no avail?

Ancient Path

Be mindful of your mercy, O LORD,
and of your steadfast love,
for they have been from of old.

PSALM 25:6 NRSV

Lord, reveal your kindness in my life today. You have never changed from your merciful ways; your love is as abundant as your endless existence. You are the joy I long for and the mercy that frees me from every trap of the enemy. Your faithful love is the constant thread through creation. I will not be afraid of failure with your redemption as my safe guard at every point. Even when things fall apart and there seems to be no hope, you are always bringing new life out of the ashes.

You've seen how my heart vacillates in faith and that I've doubted your kindness. Nevertheless, I'm thankful that your affection is steadier than my belief. Today, fill my heart with your generous peace that calms the waves of worry. May my attention be set on you and your constant faithfulness. You are good!

*As you look through history, do you see
the thread of God's faithful character?*

New Levels

He who sits on the throne said,
"Behold, I am making all things new."
And He said, "Write, for these words
are faithful and true."

REVELATION 21:5 NASB

Faithful One, you are the same yesterday, today, and forever. Your character of mercy and kindness never change. As Creator, you weren't finished making new things when you created the universe and everything in it. You are still making things new in your redemption power! You restore what was once broken, and you redeem what seemed forever lost.

I know that you're not done working things out for good in my life. Even in the midst of sorrow and grief, I trust that you are sowing seeds of life that will produce fruit. Though I cannot see evidence of it yet, I trust that you are doing the unseen work of redemption. May my heart trust your loyal love to carry me through the hard times; you haven't left me to wallow in my sorrow without comfort. Be near, Lord, and reveal yourself even in the midst of suffering.

How have you seen God turn around devastation before?

He Knows

He was despised and rejected by men,
a man of sorrows and acquainted with grief;
and as one from whom men hide their faces he was
despised, and we esteemed him not.

ISAIAH 53:3 ESV

Lord, you are the strength of my heart and my courage when nothing else remains. Grief taxes the soul and drains the energy of normal capacity. When I have nothing to offer but my actual existence, comfort me and strengthen me in your grace. I don't need to give what I don't have; neither do I need to pretend to be in a different emotional state than I am. I lean into the camaraderie of your comfort that both knows the depths of grief and has the ability to relieve it.

I'm thankful to be seen and known completely by a loving and gracious Father. Your love is beyond any others I have ever known; you are perfect in your care for me and you never disappoint. You don't miss the mark of what I need; you know exactly how to meet me in a way that alleviates the tension of despair. You always prove better than my expectations and wildest hopes. Do it again, Lord.

*Have you been completely open with the Lord
about your grief?*

Encouragement for Today

Everything that was written in the past was written
to teach us. The Scriptures give us patience and
encouragement so that we can have hope.

ROMANS 15:4 NCV

Present One, you are where all my hopes find their
fulfillment. There isn't an unspoken prayer that you haven't
heard, nor a longing in my heart that has gone unnoticed.
Your capacity is abundantly beyond any I could ever
imagine. You counsel in kindness and comfort, and you
never leave me to my own devices when I ask for your help.

May I find comfort and courage in your Word today that
meets me precisely where I am. Enlighten my mind with
your truth that causes the embers of faith to blow into
flames. You are the one who keeps my heart steady as I
walk through the winding road of life. You hold my hand
and guide me through the unknown, and I find rest in trust,
knowing that you always see clearly. You know the way
we're going, and you see everything ahead. Lead on, Lord.

*What was the last thing that really spoke to you
from God's Word?*

Not in Vain

LORD, you know the hopes of the helpless.
Surely you will hear their cries and comfort them.

PSALM 10:17 NLT

Holy Lord, in power you hold all things together. You never abandon the helpless or leave the weak to fight for themselves. You clearly see my weakness today and the hesitations of my heart. Answer the cries that rise up to you from my soul; I need you more than I can even verbalize. Be my close comfort and the lifter of my head. You are the only one who has proven faithful to always come through. Don't stop showing up in your love.

Holy Spirit, fill me with the peace of your presence. I have known the satisfaction of your nearness; let my heart be assured of you as my present comfort once again. I rely on you to help me in ways that only you can. Give me courage where there is worry, peace for anxiety, and a clear mind where my thoughts are racing. You've done it before; show up in power again.

What is the posture of your heart toward the Lord today?

Over and Over

Our fathers who were delivered from Egypt
didn't fully understand your wonders,
and they took you for granted.
Over and over you showed them
such tender love and mercy!

PSALM 106:7 TPT

Father of Lights, you were in the beginning of time; you will be faithful until the end of this age has come, and on into eternity. There isn't a day where you check out and there won't ever be a moment where you are not involved in the redemption of your people. You are continually weaving the thread of faithful love through every life that is yours. May my heart take courage in your faithfulness, and may it be strengthened in your presence.

May I not be known as one that took you for granted. Your presence is my peace, my strength, and my joy. Even in the dark valleys of suffering, you are there, holding me up and getting me through. You comfort the wounded and heal the afflicted. I will never be alone—rejoice, my soul in the constant affection of your good Father! May my heart remain tender toward your wonderful mercy and your generous affection.

*How has God shown you the kindness
of his heart toward you?*

Come Again

You who are my Comforter in sorrow,
my heart is faint within me.

JEREMIAH 8:18 NIV

Comforter, you see the cracks in my heart that need to be filled with your tender love and mercy. I have wearied of the sorrow that floods my system when I consider the great losses in life. When the grief is too much to bear, wrap me in the comforting embrace of your incredible love. In your affection, I find true acceptance no matter what state I am in. When I cry out for help, you are quick to come. Don't delay now.

Holy Spirit, I rely on your grace to cover and fill me. I cannot even get out of bed on my own when the agony of grief grips me. Instead of walking away from me, you come close, knowing exactly how to comfort me in the suffering of my soul. You don't offer empty platitudes or doubtful silence; your love emanates through to the depths of my soul from your persistent presence. I know that you understand. Don't let go of me; be a closer comfort than I've known up to this point.

Have you experienced the comfort of God's presence?

Unimaginable Power

He will take our weak mortal bodies and change them
into glorious bodies like his own, using the same power
with which he will bring everything under his control.

PHILIPPIANS 3:21 NLT

Powerful One, you are capable of doing what seems
impossible to the human mind. You heal the terminally ill,
raise the dead, and fix the most shattered hearts with your
unfailing love. Even now you are working in the middle of
the messes of my life to bring redemption. Fill my heart
with faith to know that you are with me through every trial
and hard circumstance. When life brings me to my knees,
lift me up in your love.

When all is said and done, you have the final say over
life and death. I will not get caught up in the details of
the mystery, but I will lean into your love, knowing that
everything you do is done in matchless love. My heart
anticipates the age to come where there will be no more
sickness or death. There will be no more weeping and no
more loss; I will know you completely then even as I am
completely known by you now. And joyous reunions await!
Oh heart, take hope.

Do you have hope for what awaits after death?

Spirit Thoughts

To set the mind on the flesh is death,
but to set the mind on the Spirit is life and peace.

ROMANS 8:6 ESV

Spirit of God, I set my mind on you today. Fill my thoughts with the fruit of your presence. May peace be my portion today, calming any racing, anxious thoughts. May patience bring clarity to my life and rest to my heart as I wait on you. In all things, may your life in mine be made clear through your constant companionship. With you as my helper, confidant and wise leader, I will never want for anything.

Where I am struggling to see your goodness in my life, shift my perspective to see as you do. When my heart feels heavy with the weight of sorrow, let your love flow in and lift off the heaviness. You are always ready to meet me with the generous mercy of your heart, and today I am desperate to know it in a new way. Flood my senses with your grace and love me to life.

Where do you see the evidence of
the fruit of the Spirit in your life?

Always Known

I will be glad and rejoice in Your mercy,
For You have considered my trouble;
You have known my soul in adversities.

PSALM 31:7 NKJV

Merciful God, you know me completely. What an amazing and humbling thought—that you really see me. You see past the façade, past the projections, and past the wounds. You see right to the core of who you created me to be, and you know exactly how to communicate your affection to me in a way that I understand. You celebrate with me in my victories, and you comfort me in the grief. Father, I am undone at the revelation of your kindness and mercy today.

When I consider your great love, and the uninhibited delight you have shown me, I can't help but say thank you. My heart rejoices in your mercy; let the words of my mouth utter the appreciation that I feel. Even when words fall short, you see. Through tears and through groans, there is the mystery of gladness mixed with mourning. I am so thankful for your love that always meets me right where I am.

Are you convinced that God accepts you just as you are today?

Abundant Provision

May mercy, peace, and love be yours in abundance.

JUDE 1:2 NRSV

Provider, in you is all I need for this life. There is no lack in you—you are the creator of this world and everything in it; you didn't just make it and then abandon us. The measure of your kingdom is always abundance. Your love is wider than the expanse of the sky and higher than the heavens. Your mercy is denser than platinum and more plentiful than sand on the shores of the sea.

Your peace is more powerful than the mightiest army the earth has ever seen. Your generous heart is always pouring out more than we could ever take in. Today, may I receive more of you as you enlarge my capacity. Out of the riches of your mercy, pour out a generous portion over my life. Give me eyes to see, ears to hear, and a heart that recognizes the move of your Spirit in every season of the soul.

Do you believe God is a God of just enough or of abundance?

Wholeness in Him

May the God who gives us his peace and wholeness be with you all. Yes, Lord, so let it be!

ROMANS 15:33 TPT

Holy One, you are the God of peace. You do not operate in chaos, but instead you bring order to everything. Where there is confusion, your presence brings the clarity of wisdom. Your lovingkindness is the imprint you leave on everything you do. Lord, bring wholeness to my life. I have been scattered and shattered, but you are the restorer of everything broken.

Breathe life into the barren places in my world. I rely on you to do it—I've done all I can, and it's never enough. But you, Lord, effortlessly move in wonders. You speak, and everything finds its rightful place. You breathe and peace brings calm and clarity to disorder. You are so much more capable of bringing beauty out of the ashes of disappointed hopes and crushed dreams than I am. I can't do such a thing, but you are a masterful restorer and redeemer.

Where do you need restoration in your life?

Life Forever

That faith and that knowledge come from the hope for
life forever, which God promised to us before time began.

TITUS 1:2 NCV

Faithful Father, I have placed all my bets on you. My life
has been yours and it still is. Today, I remind my soul that
you are the same loving God I've known up until now—in
fact, even more so! Your unfailing compassion carries me
through the darkest days; your unwavering hand guides me
through the lowest valleys. You are my hope when I have
none. You are my joy when my heart is being crushed by
sorrow. You will not let me be lost to despair. You will not
let disappointment take me out.

You are the God of Abraham, the one to whom he pledged
his life in faith. You are the God of David, who called out
to you in his despair and who praised you on the peaks of
his life. You are the God of Paul, who left his elite life as a
religious leader to follow the radical path of Jesus. You are
my God, who will prove as faithful as you ever have. You
will not leave me nor forsake me. And I will walk with you
into the light of eternal life where all fears will be forever
laid to rest.

*When you think of life, what are the hopes
that spring to mind?*

Seeds Sown

Those who sow in tears
shall reap with shouts of joy.

PSALM 126:5 ESV

God, in you I have found a reliable source of hope. Your unfailing love always follows through on your promises. You are faithful in all your ways, and your kindness knows no boundaries. When I am tempted to give up and surrender to the fear of the world and its ways, redirect me back to your path of love that paves a way straight to the heart of the Father. Where there is chaos and confusion, your peace stills with the clarity of wisdom. Where there is worry about the unknowns of the future, your love settles my heart with confidence in your constant character.

I know that nothing will go to waste. Even my sorrow and suffering will lead to the fruit of goodness. I have to believe that you are sowing your fruit of life and beauty amidst the ashes of the losses I've endured. There is no other way for me but to hope because if I don't have that, I would fall into despair. You are faithful! Your love won't stop working and you won't give up on me. Joy is coming.

*Does your heart trust God's timing
in the shifting of seasons?*

Out of My Hands

We can make our plans,
but the LORD determines our steps.

PROVERBS 16:9 NLT

Holy One, I have bound my life to yours; my heart is yours to hold. You are the leader of my life, and you guide my steps in your wisdom in every season. Though I make my plans and you encourage me to do so, you know what will work and what will fail. There isn't a situation where your grace is not sufficient. There is no circumstance where you leave me to my limited understanding. You lead me in love at every moment, even when I don't understand the twists and turns of the road I walk.

When life spins out of my perceived control, let my mind be steadied in the knowledge that your faithfulness still covers me. May my heart be confident in your leadership over my life; when worries and anxiety start to shift my focus from you to me, gently redirect my gaze back to you. You see what I cannot, and everything you do is laced with love. May my heart remember this every time my mind starts to wonder.

When you cannot control an outcome,
can you trust that God knows better?

August

I am praying to you because I know
you will answer, O God.
Bend down and listen as I pray.

PSALM 17:6 NLT

Taken Care Of

> "People everywhere seem to worry about making a living, but your heavenly Father knows your every need and will take care of you."
>
> LUKE 12:30 TPT

Provider, I am reminded through your Word today that you satisfy every need. You don't overlook any necessity; you are keenly aware of what I don't even know to ask for. Help my heart to trust when it wavers with worry. Remind me of your faithfulness when my mind starts to wander into unknown possibilities. Your hand steadies me when I distractedly trip; even when I fall, you lift me back up again.

Give me the peace of your presence that calms my anxious heart. Your presence is life to me; without it, the push and pull of the world would tear me apart. I rely on you to take care of me. It seems tedious to ask for help when I've done it a thousand times before, but I know that you don't ever grow tired of lovingly aiding your children. Here I am, your child; may I be filled with the confidence of your love and affection as I come to you over and over again.

What worries can you turn into petitions today?

Strong in Joy

Don't be sad, because the joy of the LORD
will make you strong.

NEHEMIAH 8:10 NCV

Holy One, would your love be the spring in my soul that overflows with joy? I've been running on empty; sadness has seeped the strength of my heart. But you, Lord, are never-ending in kindness and always abundantly offering your perfect love that covers every fear. I know that you don't require me to be anything other than what I am at this moment, yet you instruct me and lead me on in growth. When the healing of my heart feels like a type of dying, may I remember that it is only part of the process. Joy comes in the morning after a long, dark night.

When I'm walking through the darkness, with my hand firmly gripping yours, would you fill me with the underlying joy of your presence that is always with me? When my eyes are searching the horizon for any hint of dawn, lift my eyes to where the stars shine, giving light in the meantime. Let your presence with me be the joy that gives me strength today.

Have you experienced joy in the midst of sorrow?

Generations of Mercy

His mercy is for those who fear him
from generation to generation.

LUKE 1:50 NRSV

Yahweh, you are the same God through all of time. You are cloaked in mercy, and your features are kindness and compassion. You don't turn away a hurting heart, and you don't punish the weak. You are quick with affection and generous in patience. As I look through history, I can see the fingerprints of your mercy. As I remember my own, let me see with eyes that recognize your gracious touches throughout it.

Lord, my heart honors your faithfulness. My life is submitted to yours; let your good fruit be evident in my choices. I don't want to wander in doubt; I want to be rooted in the hopeful expectation of your goodness meeting me in every season of life. Your Word says that your love never fails; may my life not be the exception to such a grand statement. Saturate my life with your love that never lets go!

Do you see evidence of God's mercy in your life?

Steady Support

If I say, "My foot slips,"
Your mercy, O LORD, will hold me up.

PSALM 94:18 NKJV

Steady One, you are the support that I lean upon all the days of my life. When I have no strength of my own, your love fills me with everything I need. Your grace empowers me to stand when I would fall to my knees. And when I do fall, you are there to catch me. There is no end to the mercy that you show your children; what a wonderful truth that you call me your own!

With your favor over my life, I will not be overwhelmed by the fear of the unknown. I don't know how you do it, but you always make a way for revival. In your love, you bring restoration to what was destroyed. You make new life grow out of the ashes of ruin. Do it again, Lord! Don't delay in your faithfulness. Keep my heart steady as I cling to you with every ounce of strength that I have.

What kind of support system do you have in your life?

How Much More

I am weary with my sighing;
Every night I make my bed swim,
I dissolve my couch with my tears.
My eye has wasted away with grief;
It has become old because of all my adversaries.

PSALM 6:6-8 NASB

God, I don't have to tell you how grief works. You know well that I cycle into deep sorrow—sometimes expectedly and other times out of the blue. I can't hold back the tears that flood my eyes when I feel the great sorrow that loss has carved in me. I take consolation in the fact that you are acquainted with grief and suffering. You are not a stranger to its waves. As I allow myself to feel the pain of my loss, I invite your Spirit to make your nearness known.

As I weary of the grief, my heart will not remain discouraged. As you heal my heart, I will know your goodness even in the depths of pain. This is not the end, and I know you will teach me more about your love through this. My heart says "Yes, Lord."

When was the last time you gave yourself permission to engage with your grief?

Unifying Love

If there is any encouragement in Christ, any comfort from love, any participation in the Spirit, any affection and sympathy, complete my joy by being of the same mind, having the same love, being in full accord and of one mind.

PHILIPPIANS 2:1-2 ESV

Compassionate One, you are full of love, comfort, and encouragement. Oh, how my soul longs for each of those today! Shower me with your affection, surround me with your comfort, and fill me with reassurance. As I am met with the fullness of your goodness, I have more than enough to offer others. I will not hoard your love when you freely offer it. As I give to others, I know that I will receive more because you are a well that never runs dry.

Where I have felt disconnected and alone, may I be met with your love that connects and unifies. You are always better than I expect you to be; when I see the ways you provide, my heart is overcome with gratitude. May today be one for the books in the way that your love shows up. I won't overlook the extravagance of your kindness or keep it to myself.

Who can you extend compassion to today?

Consider It

If you are truly wise, you'll learn from what I've told you.
It's time for you to consider these profound lessons
of God's great love and mercy.

PSALM 107:43 TPT

Wise God, you have all the answers to every question I
could ever think to ask. You hold the solution for every
problem that arises. When I think about the questions on
my heart, I won't hold them back from you today. But I
also won't let them run rampant without giving your Spirit
permission to speak and guide me through them. Your
truth is often offensively simple—the kind of simple that
children can understand. May my heart be tuned to yours,
able to perceive the profound truth of your love. It all
comes back to that.

When I am tempted to run over others and myself with the
logic of the world, ground me in your wisdom that prefers
compassion to being right. Align my mind with yours, Lord.

What simple truths have been proven in your life lately?

Persevere

Keep yourselves in the love of God, waiting for the
mercy of our Lord Jesus Christ that leads to eternal life.

JUDE 1:21 ESV

God, here I am again turning my heart and attention
toward you. Fill me with everything I need to stay
connected in life-giving love today. In the in-between of
promise and fulfillment, keep me tucked into your love
that keeps my heart trusting in your faithfulness. May your
goodness be the thread that keeps me tied to you through
all circumstances. Don't withhold your grace that gives me
the tenacity to keep pressing on in the face of what looks
like defeat.

You are better than my best day and more fulfilling than
my greatest success. I lean into your love again. With
your love as my fuel, I can face anything. In the depths of
the unknown and in the shallows of understanding, may I
always be found in you, my gracious and good God.

What helps you keep pressing on in the face of hardship?

Once Again

*You will increase my honor,
and comfort me once again.*

PSALM 71:21 NRSV

Lord, in the depths of my despair, I call out to you. King David didn't censor himself with you, and neither will I. In every season of the soul, you remain faithful. You are the same merciful God that bestowed your kindness on the Israelites when they were wandering in the desert, providing for their every need. Your love doesn't let any circumstance go to waste. You are redeemer and restorer; I won't be put to shame when I trust in you.

As the psalmist prayed, so do I: increase my honor, Lord, and comfort me once again with your love. Lift me up from the dust of destruction and revive my heart in you yet again. You are the only hope I have; don't let me be disappointed or put to shame as I trust in you. Consider my desperation; cover me with your kindness and empower me with your strength!

What comfort do you need today?

Pure Motives

The LORD wants to show his mercy to you.
He wants to rise and comfort you.
The LORD is a fair God,
and everyone who waits for his help will be happy.

ISAIAH 30:18 NCV

Lord God, refresh my mind and my heart in you again today. Your love is stronger than the pull of this world; keep me close to you, sheltered by the mercy of your heart. When I am prone to fear and worry about the unknown, cover my mind with your peace that soothes. As I wait for you to lead me out of the dark valley of grief, I will let your faithful love be the substance of my hope.

Rise, even now, God, in your comfort once again. Meet me right where I am in this moment and give me what I need most. Only you know how to turn sorrow into joy; I trust that you are working that in me even when I can't see what you're doing. When I look back on this season, may I see that your faithful presence carried me through. Let me see the evidence of the life you're sowing in the winter of my heart. When spring comes, it will break through the soil and I will see the seeds that you planted.

Do you trust that God's intentions toward you are kind?

Every Morning

The Sovereign LORD has given me his words of wisdom,
so that I know how to comfort the weary.
Morning by morning he wakens me
and opens my understanding to his will.

ISAIAH 50:4 NLT

Sovereign Lord, be my guide and teacher today. As I look to you, would you give me the clues of your presence that point to your power at work within me? I'm grateful that I don't have to look to the past or the future to find you, though you are in it all. Here I am, and here you are. Your attention to detail is unmatched, and I yield my understanding to your instruction.

Holy Spirit, fill me anew in this moment; refresh me with the inhalation of every breath, giving me new revelations of your kindness in my life. Open my mind to your higher thoughts; your law of love supersedes the ways of this world—for that, I'm so grateful. When disappointment rocks my world and loss rips through my heart, you remain the same constant, loyal Father and friend that you have been all along. I trust that as I follow in your path of love, I will find your ways are better than any I have ever known. May I walk in your steps all the days of my life.

How has God's wisdom changed the way you live?

A Season

"Now is your time of grief,
but I will see you again and you will rejoice,
and no one will take away your joy."

JOHN 16:22 NIV

Great God, you are master of everything. There isn't anything that you can't do, and there is no area where you lack in understanding. As I refocus my attention on you today, I ask for your power to be made evident in my life. You see me on my best days and on my worst; you love me the same through all of them. You are never surprised by my actions or by my lack of understanding. It is impossible for me to understand the length of your patience and kindness, but I want to know you more.

In my grief, be my present and strong help. Hold me in the comforting embrace of your love and restore my heart even while it's breaking. I know that sorrow won't last forever, though it is taxing on my hope. I believe that I will see you and know you as I am fully known. May my heart know your joy now, Lord. Restore my vision and give me a glimpse of your goodness in my present reality.

What season of the soul are you in right now?

Rejoicing in Comfort

Sing for joy, O heavens, and exult, O earth;
break forth, O mountains, into singing!
For the LORD has comforted his people,
and will have compassion on his suffering one.

ISAIAH 49:13 NRSV

Comforter, you are close to all who mourn; you are near to the brokenhearted. I have known your comfort in my life, and you are nothing if not consistent. I need to know the nearness of your merciful presence again. You know how quickly I can start to waver in doubt. Though I hesitate to admit it, it's true. Come near again and show me your incredible compassion.

Though I have seen how you show up, I want to see more. Though I have heard of how you heal, I want to experience it more. No matter how many times I fall or how many times I suffer, you are always willing to pick me up and minister healing to me. Let my heart rejoice in your nearness today; don't hesitate or delay. You're all I depend upon—you're where my hopes lie!

When you receive comfort, what does it do to your heart?

My Protection

The name of the Lord is blessed and lifted high!
For his marvelous miracle of mercy protected me
when I was overwhelmed by my enemies.

PSALM 31:21 TPT

Good God, when I'm in the midst of trials and troubles, you are my protector. You defend me from my enemies and keep me safe under the covering of your mercy. When I am outnumbered by difficulties, you rise to my aid and help me. Let me see your miracle-working power in my life as you bring clarity to the messes I've made and bring peace to the chaos. I could never do that on my own, but you specialize in redeeming terrible situations for my good and benefit.

Where I see no glimpse of goodness in a situation, I trust that you will weave your mercy into it. When I see no way out, I rely on you to lead me in your kindness. History doesn't favor the strong but the brave. May my heart know courage as I press into you. Keep me steady in your love and I will make it through anything.

How have you recognized God's protection over your life?

Timing

For every matter there is a time and judgment,
Though the misery of man increases greatly.

ECCLESIASTES 8:6 NKJV

Gracious God, in you is all the wisdom that the world searches for. My heart has known confidence, both vainly in my youth and with the tenacity of faith that relies on your ability and nature. But when my heart wavers in belief, you remain constant and true through every season and through every age. You cannot be convinced out of your mercy or forced to abandon your kindness.

Lord, look at my life and the state I'm in right now. You see me just as I am, with the capacity of a child. Guide me and teach me as I look to you. You will judge everything rightly and fairly. You have the wisdom to do it and do it you will. May my heart be linked to yours in love as time draws on. Instead of taking matters into my own hands, may my heart rest in your perfect timing and righteous wisdom. You always know better.

Have you been impatient with God's timing?

More Than Able

"I know that You can do all things,
And that no purpose of Yours can be thwarted."

JOB 42:2 NASB

Righteous One, I turn my heart toward you right here and now. In faith, I have offered my life to you more than once, inviting you to lead me on your pathway of peace. Yielding to you is a habit of continually turning to you; may my heart not weary in the practice of it. I set my attention on your mercy today and offer you my mind. Direct me toward your goodness that is always present within my story. You have not led me this far in life to abandon me. You will not leave me to a sinking ship in the middle of a stormy ocean of loss.

Restore hope and joy out of the ashes of despair and grief. You have set your intentions long before I came along, and they are born out of the kindness and compassion of your heart. What you have set in motion, no man or power can deter. Have your way in my life and lead me on in mercy!

What seems impossible in your life right now?

Not Forgotten

"Can a woman forget the baby she nurses?
Can she feel no kindness for the child
to which she gave birth?
Even if she could forget her children,
I will not forget you."

ISAIAH 49:15 NCV

Loving Lord, you are watchful of your children and attentive to their cries. When I call out to you, you come to my rescue every single time. You are more caring than the most devoted mother. I don't need to worry whether you will take care of me when I am helpless; you always do. May I know the kindness of your affection toward me today; draw me close again with your tender love.

My heart is encouraged by the compassion you continually cover me in. I cannot wander outside of the length of your love; you are with me wherever I go. Like a dearly loved child, I run into your arms today. I do not need to have an agenda—you don't! I simply come because I am yours.

Have you experienced God's tender care for you?

Discernment

The wise see danger ahead and avoid it,
but fools keep going and get into trouble.

PROVERBS 27:12 NCV

Holy God, you are the standard I set my life against. It is your wisdom that guides me through the twists and turns of life. I'm so grateful that I don't need to depend on my own understanding because it so often fails me. As I live my life, following you on your pathway of peace, I will find that your goodness rises up to meet me in every season. Even when it is not easily discernable in the moment, I know that you never let anything go to waste. In what looks like destruction, I know that you bring new life out of the ashes.

Lord, where there are troubles that are avoidable, direct my steps according to your mercy. As I submit myself to you and your truth, I open myself to godly counsel with trusted friends and mentors. I know that in the counsel of many, there is wisdom. May I have the discernment to avoid the pitfalls of foolishness; I rely on your insight more than any other.

*Have you been making decisions in isolation
or seeking godly wisdom?*

Growing

Let us stop going over the basic teachings about Christ again and again. Let us go on instead and become mature in our understanding. Surely we don't need to start again with the fundamental importance of repenting from evil deeds and placing our faith in God.

HEBREWS 6:1 NLT

Giver of life, you are the source of every living thing. When things are good, it is easy to point to you and say what a good God you are. When walking through the shadowy valley of death and darkness, it is much easier to question your sovereignty. But you never ever change. Your mercy is the mark you leave in every season. You don't withdraw your presence from those who seek you.

Today, Lord, as I walk with you, may my heart continue to grow in the garden of your grace. May I have the wisdom and understanding of one who is growing up in you. With the foundation of your love as the rock beneath my feet, I don't need to keep questioning whether I am accepted by you. Lead me on and teach me more of your mysterious ways.

Where are you in your faith journey?

Pressing On

You need to persevere so that when you have done the will of God, you will receive what he has promised.

HEBREWS 10:36 NIV

Faithful Father, when the going gets tough, I do one of two things. I either press in and keep rolling right through it, or I get overwhelmed and stop doing much of anything worthwhile. I know that you are loyal in your love, and you never give up or give in. You also don't ignore the realities that I face. I press my heart into yours today, and I focus my attention on you, my good, good God!

You are so consistent in your love. May my heart find courage to persevere as I drink from your waters of grace each new day. Even as I rest in your presence, may my soul find the resolve it needs to keep pressing on, no matter what I'm facing. I rely on your generous goodness today as my source of strength. May I not give up on you; I know that you won't ever give up on me!

How can you choose to persevere today?

Greater Love

Don't set the affections of your heart on this world or in loving the things of the world. The love of the Father and the love of the world are incompatible.

1 John 2:15 TPT

Lord, you know how my heart is drawn toward lovely things. There is so much in this world that I admire and long after; my imagination is enticed by the possibility of what could be. But you are so much better than anything my eyes can see. Where my heart longs for love and acceptance from those around me, you freely offer it. The purity of your love, without condition or spin, is absolutely unmatched in any other person.

Where the love of the world is never satisfied—always wanting more, bigger, better—your love gratifies to the depths of the soul. May my heart find pleasure in your unmarred affection. You don't play games with me or require me to be anything other than who I am. What a love! Even now, let the radiance of your very present love illuminate my soul with the abundance of your goodness. There is no one else like you.

What have you been setting your affections and longings on?

Made New

Create in me a clean heart, O God,
and put a new and right spirit within me.

PSALM 51:10 NRSV

Merciful God, I come to you with the true state of my heart today. The jumble of emotions and conflicting thoughts are yours to untangle. I cannot get myself to a place of peace today. Only your Spirit can do that. I offer myself to you fully again. Would you renew me today with your lifegiving presence? Breathe on me, oh whisper of God. Revive my heart in the refreshing waters of your kindness and truth.

As the psalmist prayed, so do I: fashion in me a pure heart and put a right spirit within me. You wash over me with the waterfall of your mercy, and you make me new. Your redemption and restoration are always extended toward your children. There is never a heart too hard, never a situation too dire that you can't turn it around. Thank you, God! All of my hopes are set on you, and you won't disappoint.

When was the last time your heart and mind felt clear?

Source

All things are of God,
who has reconciled us to Himself through Jesus Christ,
and has given us the ministry of reconciliation.

2 CORINTHIANS 5:18 NKJV

Good God, I align my life with you. Let your mercy put everything that's out of place into its rightful spot in you. Your perspective is perfect, and it is your wisdom I rely on. My own limited and faulty understanding gets me so far, but I know that your eyes take everything into consideration. Knowing your faithful and kind nature never falters, I trust that you will do what I could never do and bring life out of the ruins of my broken expectations.

Where doubt, confusion, and pain have dug ravines within the landscape of my soul, I ask that you would fill them with your waters of love. You have everything I'll ever need to not just get through life, but to experience it with joy, peace, and the power of your presence. It is that power that I invite into my experience today; empower me to life today, Lord. Bring hope where I could see none even moments ago. I trust in you.

What do you need from God today?

Good Food

"Don't work for the food that spoils. Work for the food that stays good always and gives eternal life. The Son of Man will give you this food, because on him God the Father has put his power."

JOHN 6:27 NCV

Lord, as I look to you today, would you refocus my eyes on the things that matter? Where I have gotten caught up in the unnecessary details of my existence, would you help me to pan out to your wider perspective? May I see through the lens of your love that takes all things into consideration. I come to your table of plenty to feast on your wonderful character. Your peace and joy are mine for the taking. I receive your good food that satiates in a way that nothing else does.

May the fruit of my life be consistent with your kingdom, God. There is no law against compassion, mercy, or love. Let my life be full of these as I draw from the never-ending well of your presence. Though I have tasted and seen your goodness in this life, I know that it does not compare to the goodness that awaits us in your unhindered glory. What a hope!

What have you been putting the majority of your energy toward?

Greater Understanding

How blessed is the man who finds wisdom
And the man who gains understanding.

PROVERBS 3:13 NASB

Wise One, your perspective is perfect. You see and know everything there is to know; there are no mysteries to you. Why would I rely on my own inadequate understanding when I have access to your unmatched wisdom? I won't be swept away by the theories of proud people; I test everything according to your Word that guides me. The fruit of wisdom is life and peace.

May my heart rest in trust as you guide me along the path of life. You lead me in love and understanding, and my own will grow as I spend time getting to know you more. A lifetime spent knowing and being known by you is one well lived. May I remember that when I start to get tripped up by the rises and dips of success and failure. In every moment, may I find my purpose in you, God. Let all lesser things fade into the background.

How do you know that you've found wisdom?

Not My Way

Going a little farther, he fell on the ground and prayed
that, if it were possible, the hour might pass from him.
And he said, "Abba, Father, all things are possible for
you. Remove this cup from me. Yet not what I will,
but what you will."

MARK 14:35–36 ESV

Jesus, I am so grateful to know that you experienced the
reality of the spectrum of emotions in life. In subjecting
yourself to the limited, human experience, you felt
exhilaration and you felt desperation. There isn't anything I
face that you did not also come face-to-face with in some
form. You felt the pangs of loss, the joy of laughing with
friends, and the longing of what was yet to come.

In the garden of Gethsemane, you pled with the Father to
allow your life to be spared, and in the end submitted your
will to his. Lord, as I struggle through facing what comes,
my desperate heart often cries out to you. Let my heart
always end up where yours did, with submission and trust
in God the Father. Thank you for the understanding you
have of pain and suffering; as I walk through sorrow, I invite
you into it. May I find comfort in your solidarity today.

When faced with unfavorable circumstances,
are you able to get to a place of surrender and trust?

Victorious Life

I have saved these most important truths for last: Be supernaturally infused with strength through your life-union with the Lord Jesus. Stand victorious with the force of his explosive power flowing in and through you.

EPHESIANS 6:10 TPT

Holy One, it is through my relationship with you that I have everything I need for anything I face. You are not just a storehouse of supplies for my life; you aren't like some distant grandfather doling out gifts according to how well pleased you are with people at any given time. You are a very present friend, help, teacher, and Father. You are closer than the breath in my lungs and more powerful than all of the weapons of the world put together.

Your nature is kindhearted and you are merciful to all those who come to you. Today and everyday may I be infused with your strength. My life is yours, united with you. Your power is present; I don't have to go looking for it. Lord, astound me with the goodness that comes from your nearness. Revive my heart in the incubator of your love. Lead me into abundance of life as I lean into you.

What does it mean to live with victory?

Leader of my Life

Whether you turn to the right or to the left,
your ears will hear a voice behind you, saying,
"This is the way; walk in it."

ISAIAH 30:21 NIV

Shepherd of my soul, I depend on you to guide me through this life. I have been relying on your wisdom up until this point, and I won't stop now. May I walk in the pathway of your peace all the days of my life, trusting you to guide me through all the twists and turns. I know that even when I am surprised by unexpected happenings, you never are. I trust that you will keep me close and keep me safe in your love.

My plans have been disrupted more than once in life. But you, God, have led me through the mountains and the valleys with goodness. Even when I could not see a way out of the dark caverns, you always faithfully guided me through them. I know that you won't stop now. I lean on your love and depend on your mercy to keep leading me. Have your way and keep me steady when I falter.

Do you trust God to lead you in your decisions?

No More Pain

"He will wipe every tear from their eyes,
and there will be no more death
or sorrow or crying or pain.
All these things are gone forever."

REVELATION 21:4 NLT

Prince of Peace, how my heart longs for the day when every tear will dry and death, pain, and sorrow will be a distant memory. For now, I set my hope on you, the sustainer of my faith and my very life. I can't understand the depths of the sorrow that I'm walking through, but I know that you are with me. Let that be enough for now.

Minister your healing to my heart through the tender nearness of your Spirit. Your presence is what holds me together. As I wade through the pain of loss, keep me anchored in your love. As I try to imagine a life with no weeping or despair, may my heart catch a glimpse of your coming kingdom. Be my very present peace in the midst of the emotional storms and steady me with your merciful hand. I need you more than I can express.

*How does your heart respond to
the thought of God's coming kingdom?*

Follow Through

The plans of the diligent lead surely to plenty,
But those of everyone who is hasty, surely to poverty.

PROVERBS 21:5 NKJV

Faithful One, as I walk this road of life with you, I depend on your strength to be my own. My good intentions only go so far. Would you lead me in your wisdom that helps me to prioritize well and keep my word? I won't ever get it perfect, but I can surely get it right some of the time. You, Lord, are consistent in kindness and mercy. You always fulfill your promises. May my life reflect yours in constancy and in perseverance.

Lord, help me to be wise in what I say yes to. Where haste leads to impulsive decisions, your wisdom takes more than just the moment into consideration. Give me temperance where I am prone to rush. I know that your ways are better than my own; may my life be aligned with yours. Thank you for grace that covers my mistakes and mercy that helps me to start fresh when needed. Let shame and guilt be far from me so I can keep moving in you.

Where are you prone to hasty decisions?

Architect

It is by faith we understand that the whole world was made by God's command so what we see was made by something that cannot be seen.

HEBREWS 11:3 NCV

Creator, you are the master maker of all things. In areas where I think I know better than you how things should go, would you gently put me back in my place? I only see in part (and a tiny one, at that!), but you see the whole picture from end to end and all the spaces in between. May my heart take courage in trusting you and your ways, knowing that you've got this. I can't control how things will turn out; I can only do my best and trust you with the rest.

Where my heart is clinging to expected or hopeful outcomes, will you help me to let go? You are the source of all life, and you don't waste anything. May my heart rest in your higher wisdom and your ability to redeem and restore. Calm the chaos in my head and bring clarity as I choose to believe that you are good—so much better, in fact, than I could ever imagine. Have your way, Lord; I loosen my grip today.

What have you been holding onto too tightly?

September

"Keep watch and pray,
so that you will not give in to temptation.
For the spirit is willing,
but the body is weak!"

MATTHEW 26:41 NLT

Patience

The Lord is not slow about His promise, as some count slowness, but is patient toward you, not wishing for any to perish but for all to come to repentance.

2 PETER 3:9 NASB

Lord God, your wisdom is above my own understanding. As I meditate on your Word, my heart aligns with your truth that is higher than the laws that hold the universe together. You never overlook a detail, and you never miss an opportunity to extend your mercy. Let my heart rest in your peace today, trusting that you won't forget to fulfill every promise you have made.

Your faithfulness is more reliable than the rising and ebbing of the tides; your love is more loyal than the sunrise. When I consider the seasons of the earth and the way nature responds to the shifts, I can't help but hope for the fruit-bearing seasons to hurry up. Give my heart proper perspective that I wouldn't despise the decay of autumn or the dormancy of winter. In all things, and through all seasons, your love is constant and close.

How can you practice contentment in waiting?

Giver of Life

"You gave me life and showed me kindness,
and in your providence watched over my spirit."

JOB 10:12 NIV

Creator, as you breathed life into man in the beginning, my very life is dependent on your kindness. Quiet my soul in your love and revive my heart with your Spirit. I know that every difficulty I face is an opportunity to see you in a new way. Your love won't ever let go of me, and your mercy will not leave me. Continue to watch over me all the days of my life.

Today, be the source of the strength I so desperately need. Show me your kindness again as you empower me to trust in your unfailing love. Carry me through the valley of heartache and lift me above the crags of disappointment and despair. When my heart is weak in faith, you are the same powerful God; would you redirect my gaze and readjust my perspective to see your life and compassion when all I feel is darkness and doubt? I trust you, God. Don't let me drown in the river of sadness. Keep my head above the water!

How has God shown you kindness?

Unshakable

Let us be thankful, because we have a kingdom that cannot be shaken. We should worship God in a way that pleases him with respect and fear.

HEBREWS 12:28 NCV

Mighty God, when you speak, the earth responds. When your winds of peace blow over a nation, chaos is calmed and people find rest. Your Word is the first and last—it is the ultimate authority by which heaven, earth, and everything within them find their place. Lord, when I am just going through the motions of honoring you in front of others, bring me back into alignment with you. It is not what is done in public that matters but how my heart is attuned to you when no one else knows.

Let the attitude of my heart forever be malleable by your Spirit. Your kingdom is full of love, joy, peace, kindness, gentleness, and respect. May my life be full of the same. Against these things nothing can stand; though brute strength may go a ways, the strength of a loving and submissive heart is much more potent. Your love changes everything, Lord. It is the foundation of my very life.

How do you view God's power—is it his ability to create or destroy, or is it the way he chooses to love at all cost?

Be Open

Whoever conceals his transgressions will not prosper,
but he who confesses and forsakes them
will obtain mercy.

PROVERBS 28:13 ESV

Merciful One, here is my heart, laid out like an open book before you. I have nothing to hide, and even if I did, you already know what lies in every crack and crevice. I will not choose to keep anything from you. You are rich in mercy and lavish in love; when I am vulnerable with you, you meet me with kindness. You don't ever shame me into submission; you don't lacerate me for my wrongdoings.

I come to you freely without hesitation because I know what you are like. You are kind and compassionate; even in correction your words are laced with love. You do nothing out of spite; you don't ever kick me when I'm down. You are a perfect parent, and you won't ever turn me away when I come to you. I won't come away from an encounter with you disappointed. So today, Lord, as I confess my heart to you, strengthen me in your love once again.

What have you been avoiding bringing up with the Lord?

Treasure

Your laws are my treasure;
they are my heart's delight.

PSALM 119:111 NLT

King of kings, you guide me in wisdom and truth. You lead in love in all that you do. Your example is the ultimate expression of mercy. When I follow your example, I will not fail. As I press into your nature, I will become more and more like you. As I take on your likeness, I will reflect your compassion in my life. As I reflect your compassion, kindness will be a ready response to those around me.

In all I do, may my life be attuned to your goodness and compassion. You consistently cover me with your mercy; I am nowhere near perfect nor will I ever be. Perfection isn't even on the table—it's not a requirement you give. As I follow in your way of love, I find that forgiveness, mercy, and perseverance are traits that mark my journey. I find delight along your path of life that continually teaches me to choose love over offense, pride, and judgment. And when I walk through darkness, there are even more beautiful treasures to be found.

What treasures have you found in following God's ways?

Compassionate Heart

"Show mercy and compassion for others,
just as your heavenly Father overflows
with mercy and compassion for all."

LUKE 6:36 TPT

Gracious God, as I follow you through this life, may my heart become enlarged with your love. As I practice offering the same mercy I've received, may my capacity grow. As I choose to treat others with compassion, I know that I am following your way of life. Jesus, as I look to your example, I see how these traits marked your ministry. You never turned away a hungry heart, no matter the package it came in. In kindness, you brought the heart of the Father to the people outside the walls of religion.

In the same way today, Lord, I know that you still work in love. Your compassion is unending and your mercy is impartial. I have been on the receiving end of your kindness, and here I am still. When I have opportunity, let me be quick to love and even quicker to lay down judgment and preference. May your heart of compassion flow into my own; give me eyes to see others as you do. You see the pain that we all walk through. Let me not forget that life's struggles touch us all.

*When you are faced with frustrating people,
can you choose to offer them compassion?*

Law of Love

"Do to others what you want them to do to you.
This is the meaning of the law of Moses
and the teaching of the prophets."

MATTHEW 7:12 NCV

Loving Lord, you are the barometer of justice in this world. It is not my job to put anyone in their place; in fact, when it comes to others, you are very clear that your people are to exhibit the kind of love they would like to receive. It is with unmerited kindness that I have been shown mercy. Let my heart reflect that same kindness. You are full of compassion toward your children; may I also be full of compassion.

Holy Spirit, fill me with your living water of love again today, that I may give out of the overflow of your affection. Give me eyes to see others as they are, not as inconveniences or as objects of frustration. We all walk through suffering and pain at some point; may my heart be tender and give others the benefit of the doubt. In my own sorrow, I know that I cannot always present my best to others. May there be grace all around.

*How do you treat others who
don't seem to have it together?*

It's Certain

Certainly God has heard me;
He has attended to the voice of my prayer.

PSALM 66:19 NKJV

Good God, you hear me every time I call on you. Whether it's with a whisper, or a shout, or even the unspoken prayers of my heart, you pay attention to my cries. You don't miss a single need; you don't ignore the desires of my heart. I'm grateful that I don't have to guess whether I'm heard or not; you faithfully answer me and come to my aid.

Lord, just as the sun rises in the east and sets in the west, so you come through for your children in their time of need. You are my sustainer and my hope. Even when I cannot see a foot into my future, you already know the way you are leading me. There are no surprises to you, and though you are a mystery, there are no secrets kept from you. I trust your wisdom to be my guide. Infuse my heart with courage and confidence today.

Do you trust that God hears you?

Deep Springs

"Because of your father's God, who helps you, because of the Almighty, who blesses you with blessings of the skies above, blessings of the deep springs below, blessings of the breast and womb."

GENESIS 49:25 NIV

Almighty, in you is the wealth of wisdom and every treasure ever conceived. You are a constant help in times of trouble, and you are reliable in mercy whenever I need it. There isn't a situation that isn't covered by your love; there is no pain too great that you won't heal with your comforting peace. Every imaginable blessing is found in your presence.

Holy Spirit, lead me to the deep springs of mercy today. I want to be washed in the waterfall of God's kindness. You see where I am dry and parched, desperate for your living waters to quench my thirst. Come with the abundance of your love and flood my borders with your compassion. I am yours; let my heart be met with the feast of your generous affection today.

When was the last time you felt satisfied in God's presence?

Rest in Hope

"You will have confidence, because there is hope;
you will be protected and take your rest in safety."

JOB 11:18 NRSV

God my refuge, I take shelter in you today. When the storms of life rage, I run into the sanctuary of your presence. You are my help and you are my defender. No matter the worries that have been weighing on my mind, you are more than able to take care of me. Your unfailing love covers me all the days of my life. Let your mercy be my protection as I trust in you.

Though I walk through many trials, your love never abandons me. You are faithful to come through as my faithful leader and the victor in every circumstance. Even failure can't stop me because you are a master redeemer— you somehow plant seeds of goodness in every situation, and I watch the fruit of it grow later on. I won't be afraid because you are with me. I won't lose hope because you are endlessly loyal. My confidence is in you, God. Your nature and your faithfulness are consistent. I lean into you and find my rest today.

*Can you find rest in God even
in the midst of chaos in your life?*

Forever Good

Jesus Christ is the same yesterday
and today and forever.

HEBREWS 13:8 NASB

Jesus, you are constant in love and mercy. You who humbly laid down your throne in heaven and your life in love are the same gracious man that sits at the right hand of the Father today. Father, Son, and Spirit are unified and perfect in mercy and love. As I look to your life, Jesus, I find that you always pursued the forgotten and were quick to call out truth instead of bias. You were not exclusive in who you chose to share your message of love with. You chose the normal to follow you not the religious elite.

Lord, as I follow after you, I am humbled to be yours. I am also relieved to know that you never expect perfection from me, and you certainly don't want me to pretend to be someone that I'm not. As I live my life in your presence, I continually find that you are transforming me to be more like you—to love more like you. May my heart be a sponge for your compassion and mercy, so when life squeezes me, your love would come out.

Who do you know Jesus to be?

Tenacity

Remember to stay alert and hold firmly to all that you believe. Be mighty and full of courage.

1 CORINTHIANS 16:13 TPT

Mighty God, I link my life to yours, depending on your strength and not my own. May my heart be full of your grace that empowers me to stand when the winds of adversity blow. And when I have no power of my own left, hold me up with your mercy. Today I am reminded that life doesn't just happen to me; I get to partner with you in how I get through. I won't throw my hands up in the air and surrender to the storm—I surrender to you, the voice that calms the storm!

Fill my mind with your peace that brings clarity and sharpens my focus. Let my heart rest in trust as you lead me. I am so thankful that I am not alone today, nor will I be tomorrow. You are with me, holding onto me. How could I not be filled with courage when I know that the God over all the universe is for me? You are my firm hope. As you hold onto me, I hold onto you.

When did you see God's faithful help get you through something that seemed impossibly hard?

Lean on Others

Confess your sins to each other and pray for each other so that you may be healed. The earnest prayer of a righteous person has great power and produces wonderful results.

JAMES 5:16 NLT

Wonderful Counselor, it is in your mercy that my heart has found its home. It is in your family that I have found strength and comfort to keep going. When I am discouraged and would rather isolate myself, would you remind me of the power of community? I know that you are a perfect parent, and you lead and direct me in your kindness. May my heart be encouraged as I meet kindred spirits who know you and are following you along your path of love.

Give me courage to share my victories and disappointments with those I am journeying along this life with. For those I know that love you and love me, may I be open. May we be like iron sharpening iron, encouraging each other in the faith and in life. Lord, bring to mind who I can connect with about what I'm going through. You are faithful to provide for everything—even friends and family. Thank you for relationship, Lord!

Who are your reliable and trustworthy friends that you can be open with?

Fullness of Life

You make known to me the path of life;
in your presence there is fullness of joy;
at your right hand are pleasures forevermore.

PSALM 16:11 ESV

Lord God, you are infinitely wise in your leadership. You guide me along your pathway of love that leads to life. You shine the light of your presence over me and I am filled with joy. You give out of the abundance of your kingdom gifts that satisfy the longings of my heart. Who else is there like you? What you give is unlike any other—peace that lasts, love that purifies, and wisdom that honors.

May I walk with you all the days of my life. When I stumble, or when I start to stray, lift me up and straighten me out. I know that you lead in kindness, and you correct in gentleness. Everything you do brings me life. If all I can see are questions and I am wondering when I will feel the joy of your presence again, I trust that the time is coming. You have given the keys to fullness, and I will walk in it as long as I'm walking with you.

*Do you trust God to lead you even when
you are struggling to hope?*

Vulnerability

For Christ's sake, I delight in weaknesses, in insults,
in hardships, in persecutions, in difficulties.
For when I am weak, then I am strong.

2 Corinthians 12:10 niv

Lord, I don't know that I can echo Paul's statement of delighting in weakness and the like. But I have known your power in my weakness; I have experienced your strength in my frailty. Though I don't enjoy having nothing to offer, I recognize that my worth does not rely on what I do. It is completely contingent upon your estimation of me. What a wonder, that whatever state I am in, you completely and affectionately embrace me as your own. I am loved because you love me. You love me because you are love. There is no off switch, no pause button, and no exceptions. You love me.

As I walk through the sorrow of loss, some days I can function, and others I'm completely useless. My heart is comforted by the knowledge that you love me the same regardless. Thank you for that assurance today. I rest in your love, Lord, and I let go of the expectations I cannot meet in myself.

Have you been putting pressure on yourself to be in a different emotional place than you are?

In the Meantime

It is not yet time for the message to come true, but that time is coming soon; the message will come true. It may seem like a long time, but be patient and wait for it, because it will surely come; it will not be delayed.

HABAKKUK 3:2 NCV

Holy One, in the waiting times in life, it can be difficult to not grow discouraged. In the early days of hope, it seems easy to believe. But when the days turn into weeks, turn into months, turn into years, the heart wavers in believing. When I am tempted to just give up, calling the hopes vain or foolish, would you remind me that your promises never fail? You were faithful to give Abraham and Sarah a son, though it took much longer than either expected.

My timing is not your timing; I remember that again today. May I rest in your goodness and the tangible peace of your presence as the assurance of your promise. Your Word depends on you and not on me. I want to hold onto hope that solidifies as faith in my heart. Just as Abraham's faith in you was credited to him as righteousness, may my heart stay strong in believing your promises.

Has the waiting worn you down?

Pursue Peace

Let us pursue the things which make for peace and the things by which one may edify another.

ROMANS 14:19 NKJV

Faithful Father, your love unifies, it does not tear apart. Rather than drawing a line in the sand, your love welcomes us in with peace. In the same way, may the intentions of my heart seek to unify in love and not divide in differences. You are so much better than the rulers and kingdoms of this world. You do not belittle or betray anyone with your power. You don't abandon the weak or encourage your people to fight for you. You are capable of doing anything with your authority, but you never wield it to harm.

May I live a life that reflects your same love, Lord. Where people seek to tear each other down in order to build their own ideals up, may I not give into the game. May I be full of compassion, peace, and wisdom with and for all. Only you can make that kind of fruit grow—do it in my life, Lord.

How can you be a peace-bringer today?

Reliability Matters

"He who is faithful in a very little thing is faithful also in much; and he who is unrighteous in a very little thing is unrighteous also in much."

LUKE 16:10 NASB

Gracious God, you are endlessly faithful. You always come through on your promises, and you fulfill every intention you set. I cannot pretend to have the same perfect traits, but I do want to be like you in reliability. As I choose you, and I choose to offer myself to your love over and over again, you transform me into your likeness. Even when all is dark and I cannot see a way out of the valley I'm in, I know that your faithfulness still leads me. May my heart remain pure in love as I am covered by your great affection.

Overtake every fear that keeps me from following wholeheartedly after you, Lord. You are perfect in love and you are wonderful in mercy. I can never match that but I don't need to because I am perfected by your love, not my own. Give me eyes to stay faithful in the small things of life, that I wouldn't be focused on the mountaintops but every step that leads me there.

What promise can you keep for yourself and for God today?

Invitation

He said, "Come." And when Peter had come down out of the boat, he walked on the water to go to Jesus.

MATTHEW 14:29 NKJV

Lord, when you invite me into the unknown, especially what seems scary and impossible, may I trust that the one who calls me is also the one who is with me. With his eyes fixed on you, Peter walked on water. With my eyes fixed on you, I can do anything. Let my gaze stay tuned into yours so I don't begin to sink into the worries of the troubles I am tramping on. When I do start to sink, as soon as I call out for help, you are there, lifting me up.

I recognize that I can't stay in my comfort zone and expect to grow. Lord, fear is like a wall that closes me in. May I be so consumed with your amazing character, knowing that the one who loves me perfectly will not let me drown, that I step into the unknown with you. You are worthy of my trust.

Where do you feel the pull of God inviting you into the unknown?

Heavenly Citizens

We are citizens of heaven, where the Lord Jesus Christ lives. And we are eagerly waiting for him to return as our Savior.

PHILIPPIANS 3:20 NLT

King of kings, you are the one I've pledged my life to. All my days are numbered before you—you see the span of my life, and there are no missing moments before your eyes. You see it all clearly. I won't fear with you as my wise and faithful leader. My rightful home is not this earth; this is just a temporary place until you usher in the never-ending reign of your kingdom.

When you return and make every wrong thing right, and set everything in its rightful place, your kingdom of love will reign. The peace of your presence will not have a starting point or an end; there will only be light, for you will be the sun that shines on everything. I cannot pretend that the pain of this life has not worn me down, but still, I know that there is a greater hope. And that hope is you.

What do you look forward to in the kingdom of heaven?

Lasting Peace

"Peace I leave with you; my peace I give to you.
I do not give to you as the world gives.
Do not let your hearts be troubled,
and do not let them be afraid."

JOHN 14:27 NRSV

Spirit of God, you always carry peace with your presence. When my heart begins to tremble with fear, would you breathe the breeze of your peace that calms anxiety and brings rest? You don't give your peace to take it away, yet I know that trials and troubles will threaten to disrupt the peace I carry. When that happens, may your love flood my senses, bringing everything back into order.

May my whole being be aligned with your heavenly peace, love, and joy. Today, where there is doubt, may the peace that passes understanding cover it. Where there is anxiety, may perfect love calm every nerve. Where there is despair, may your joy spring up. You are faithful to follow through; meet me with everything I need today.

When was the last time you felt true peace?

Passionate Love

Christ proved God's passionate love for us by dying in our place while we were still lost and ungodly!

ROMANS 5:8 TPT

Wonderful Lord, your fervent love is unstoppable in its intensity and intentions. Your fiery heart is reaching out to purify and restore. I cannot begin to understand the lengths that you went to in order to restore right relationship between humanity and yourself. You wanted nothing to stand in the way of your undying affection toward us. May this truth wreck me today with the revelation of your incredible, unrelenting, irresistible mercy.

A good friend might lay down his life for another, but who lays down their life for one and does not even acknowledge them? Your goodness, Jesus, is without a match in this world. You are consistently loving and kind, always pursuing with the depth of your compassion. I won't hold back from your love today; burn in me with the fiery passion of your heart.

When you consider Christ's love in laying down his life, how does your heart respond?

Not a Surprise

Do not be surprised at the fiery ordeal among you, which comes upon you for your testing, as though some strange thing were happening to you; but to the degree that you share the sufferings of Christ, keep on rejoicing, so that also at the revelation of His glory you may rejoice with exultation.

1 Peter 4:12–13 NASB

Holy One, you are the one I look to through every season of the soul. You are my help when I have no strength left. You are my confidant when I bare my heart before you. You are full of joy in celebration, and you weep with me when I am full of sorrow. You are everything I need and so much more.

God, in the times of testing and suffering, be especially near with your powerful and comforting presence. When I walk through the valley of despair, be the light that keeps me going. Life's sorrows and losses are unavoidable; they touch us all. But even in the dark night of grief, you are with me. Your sweet presence ministers healing. Be my help and give me eyes to see your perspective through it all. May I rejoice in your wonderful love in every season.

When hard times come, does your faith waver?

Humble Heart

He poured water into the basin, and began to wash the disciples' feet and to wipe them with the towel with which He was girded.

JOHN 13:5 NASB

Beautiful Lord, when you walked this earth in humility, you revealed the tender heart of the Father so clearly. Though you were a king, you laid down your crown and became like a servant to humankind. It is almost inconceivable to think that the Creator of the universe and everything within it would go incognito, clothed in flesh and bones. While the Israelites were waiting on a warrior king to rescue them from earthly governments, you came as a humble Savior— like a lamb to the slaughter.

Father, when I begin to think that I don't deserve what I'm walking through, redirect my gaze to the life of Jesus. Though you were faultless in a fallen world, you took the loving route every time. Love is costly. Choosing to continue to humble my heart before you and others is a costly act of faith. May I keep choosing you and your way.

How has pride kept you from love?

Closer

One who has unreliable friends soon comes to ruin,
but there is a friend who sticks closer than a brother.

PROVERBS 18:24 NIV

Faithful Friend, you are more loyal to me than my own flesh and blood. You are always looking out for my best even when I think I know better. As I walk with you, may the walls of offense and unbelief come toppling down under the weight of your love. Your pathway of peace is so much better than the path of pride and control. Though I often think that I know what I want, I find that your wisdom is more grounded than my own understanding that shifts with the seasons.

You are unchanging in your boundless mercy, and you are undeterred in your deep affection. Today, Lord, may I rely on your unfailing love and wisdom. You are a better friend than any I have known. You never leave, and you don't need to reevaluate your commitment toward me. Your capacity to love is unmatched. I'm so grateful to be the object of your tender care. Don't ever stop loving me to life!

How has God's friendship benefited your life?

Submitted

Instead, you ought to say,
"If the Lord wills,
we will live and also do this or that."

JAMES 4:15 NCV

Great God, I once again submit my heart and my life to you. Wherever you lead, I will follow. As I lay out my tentative plans, I keep a posture of open hands turned toward you. I trust that when you give, you give good gifts. When things fall apart, I know that you will redeem what has been lost. You know my heart that thinks it knows best much of the time; but you always know best. I submit my plans to yours, holding them loosely.

I won't despair when things don't go my way. You see every detail, and still you see the big picture. May my heart take comfort and courage in the knowledge that I can rely on you to guide me through every circumstance. Though I see in part, you see the whole. You are never worried. Fill me with the peace of your presence again today as I resubmit my will to yours.

Is there something you have been holding onto that you can surrender to God today?

Sharpened

As iron sharpens iron,
so a friend sharpens a friend.

PROVERBS 27:17 NLT

Merciful God, your very present love is.the greatest gift I have ever known. Flood my senses with your compassion in a new way today. Your friendship is the best I've ever known. You are more faithful than a brother, and more loyal than my closest friend. You see my need for fellowship in flesh and blood. You created us for companionship and for community.

Lord, remind me today of your goodness through the relationships that point to you. Whether my circle of trusted friends is small or the community I am in is large, I am thankful that there are those who encourage me to keep pressing on in you. May I not hold back from reaching out when I need it. Let those trustworthy and faithful friends be clear in my life. In your goodness, you do not set us in the wilderness of isolation but in families.

Who in your life is a trustworthy and godly influence?

Eyes Open

Since we are approaching the end of all things,
be intentional, purposeful, and self-controlled
so that you can be given to prayer.

1 PETER 4:7 TPT

Yahweh, you are purposeful in everything you set your intentions upon. Your promises are fulfilled even if the waiting seems long. As you are resolute in love, so may I be firm in faith. You are constant and unchanging; your character is unfailing. In the dark night of grieving, I will not forget your love that has never let me go. You are not done doing what you do best—restoring and redeeming.

Lord, when my eyes are straining to see you at work in my life, direct my gaze to where you are. You never leave, and you won't ever give up on me. I will not stop calling on your name; I rely on you to save me. You are my current and constant help in times of trouble. You are my strong tower and I run into you today.

Have you been coasting along lately,
or have you had moments of clear direction?

A Way Prepared

"Build up, build up, prepare the road!
Remove the obstacles out of the way of my people."

ISAIAH 57:14 NIV

Lord, I rely on you more than I can express. Does it ever get old to you that I constantly come to you with my needs? You are a kind and patient Father. You welcome me in warmly every time I approach you. May my heart be calmed by the peace of your presence again today. Lord, you have led me up until now as I've linked my life to yours; I trust that you will continue to guide me in goodness.

I can see a stark difference in the life I lived for myself, trying to make a way by hacking through the weeds. But you build a road and prepare the way. Why would I try to go my own way when you have already made a path for me to follow? Lead me on in love, Lord. I am yours.

Do you trust God to guide you through the obstacles of life?

Even So

"As for you, you meant evil against me;
but God meant it for good,
in order to bring it about as it is this day,
to save many people alive."

GENESIS 50:20 NKJV

Faithful One, my heart is bound to you in love. I belong
to you—don't abandon me to the chaos of the world that
would take me out. Even when I'm walking through the
barrenness of a winter season, I know that you are with me.
Though it seems like everything is dormant, and I struggle
to hope that the beauty of spring will ever come again,
I know that seasons don't last forever. Give my mind the
perspective it needs to trust you today.

You are the giver of life, Lord. You restore broken things
and redeem even the most vile situation with unexpected
life. You won't let the enemy trample my hopes and
you won't let me be lost to despair. You are never done
breathing life into dry bones; you always are up to
something new. May my heart take hope in your wonder-
working power.

*How have you seen God bring goodness
out of a hard situation?*

October

Answer me when I pray to you,
my God who does what is right.
Make things easier for me
when I am in trouble.
Have mercy on me and hear my prayer.

PSALM 4:1 NCV

Better than Life

Because Your lovingkindness is better than life,
My lips will praise You.

PSALM 63:3 NASB

Loving Lord, I align my heart with yours again today. Where I have gotten out of sync, line me up with your love. Your mercy is so much better than anything I could ever achieve or receive. You are lavish in lovingkindness, and you are abundant in kindness. Where I have struggled to taste and see your goodness in my life lately, may I sample and discern it clearly today.

You never give your children stones when they ask for bread; I trust that as I ask for your love to meet me today, you won't delay in pouring it out. May my senses come alive in the atmosphere of your grace. Let my mind experience the peace that passes all understanding and my heart know the fullness of your affection that breathes acceptance and relief. May my heart's response be that your love is better than life itself.

When was the last time you remember feeling the gratitude of a full heart?

Encouragement

Anxiety weighs down the human heart,
but a good word cheers it up.

PROVERBS 12:25 NRSV

Father, as I turn my attention to you today, don't hold back your affection that always welcomes me in. I am grateful that you accept me as I am—not how I think I should be. When the seeds of worry have grown into vines of anxiety, and they are creeping into the windows of my soul choking out the peace I once had, would you uproot them in your love? Clear out the weeds of worry and make space that I may breathe in the winds of your encouragement.

You are better to me than I am to myself, but as I walk with you and learn your ways, I learn to give myself the grace that you so generously offer. You are abundant in lovingkindness all the days of my life. Lift the weight of sorrow today that I may stand to see the light of life. May my heart rise to meet your love as it shines on me.

What was the last thing that cheered you up?

Only One

God is the only Lawmaker and Judge. He is the only
One who can save and destroy. So it is not right for you
to judge your neighbor.

JAMES 4:12 NCV

Holy One, you are the righteous judge. You alone are
qualified to dole out final verdicts. Your ruling no one
can contest. You show mercy to whom you show mercy
and you hold accountable those who must be held
accountable. It is your job and yours alone. Lord, I release
the judgments I have made against those who have
wronged me. I let go of the offense I've been holding in my
heart toward those who have wielded weapons that have
hurt others.

I choose to trust you and your power to save and destroy.
It is your job to judge people's hearts; it's certainly not
mine. Forgive me for the ways that I've criticized and
condemned others without your love in mind. Lord, when it
is hard for me to justify releasing responsibility, would you
give me a glimpse of your power and your mercy? I know
that you are trustworthy. I will choose to let go today and
for as long as it takes for justice to occur.

*Do you trust God enough to let him deal with those who
have hurt and offended you?*

Qualified

It is not that we think we are qualified to do anything on our own. Our qualification comes from God.

2 CORINTHIANS 3:5 NLT

God over all, you are merciful and kind. You offer me strength when I have nothing to offer at all. In my weakness, I rely on your grace to empower me to live in line with your kingdom. When I would choose the easy way, check out, and focus on myself, you offer me another way. Your mercy meets me and loves me to life. Your love has made a way out of the cocoon of shame, pain, and blame.

Lord, you are the strength of my life; everything of value that comes from me is something that you put in me in the first place. As I align my life with yours, living surrendered to your love, I find that your goodness is woven into every aspect of it. Your ways are beautiful, and the fruit of a life connected to yours is beyond anything I could dream of on my own. I know that even when I can't see it, you are working. You who called me will lead me on in grace.

Do you question whether you are able to live a life aligned with God?

Higher Thoughts

Set your minds on things that are above,
not on things that are on earth.

COLOSSIANS 3:2 NASB

Wise One, when I am drowning in the reality of loss and dashed hopes, would you be the one to lift me up? You are capable in your comfort, and you are loyal in your lovingkindness. When my thoughts are consumed by the confusion of my circumstances, breathe your peace into my mind. Bring clarity to my anxious and worried heart as I set my eyes on you.

Lord, lift my eyes when I forget that there is a different perspective. I know that your viewpoint sees everything clearly. You don't miss a thing. As I focus my attention on you, shine through the fog of worry that has kept me clouded and unable to discern your presence. You are so much better than the kindest parent; I know that I can rely on you to help me when I turn to you. May my soul be set on you; may my thoughts be grounded in the perspective of your kingdom and on your unfailing love that never lets me go.

When your mind wanders, what has it most often gone to lately?

Holy Union

"I am the Way, I am the Truth, and I am the Life. No one comes next to the Father except through union with me. To know me is to know my Father too."

JOHN 14:6 TPT

Lord God, you are the hope of every heart, even when the heart does not recognize the substance of its expectation. In union with you, I have found the belonging I never imagined could be mine. Jesus, I know that you are the way, the truth, and the life. As I walk in your way, I find peace along the path and strength through the grace that your Spirit offers. You have made a way where there was none, straight to your heart.

I am grateful to know you and be known by you; you have accepted me into your family, calling me your very own. Being loved by you is the joy of my life; it is through this communion that I have anything to offer. I have a limited supply of compassion, but yours is endless. With access to your generous heart, I lack nothing. In the abundance of your life-giving love, I have found everything I need in every season of the soul. As I have received freely, so may I also liberally offer this compassion to others.

What does union with Jesus look like in your life?

Untold Secrets

"Call to me and I will answer you, and will tell you great and hidden things that you have not known."

JEREMIAH 33:3 NRSV

Wonderful God, I won't stop calling on your name. Each new day is another opportunity to encounter your goodness and mercy in my life. With your heart of affection shining on me, I come alive to your love once again. You are infinitely good; you are better than I hope for at every turn. Even through darkness, sorrow and pain, you are with me, never withholding your love from my heart.

Lord, where I have had questions about your goodness, would you speak to me out of the wealth of your wisdom, illuminating my heart in understanding? You have so much to share, and I want to know your wonderful ways. Reveal to me what I haven't recognized before. Bring the light of revelation to shrouded mysteries. I long to know you more!

What recent revelation has changed the way you view God?

Silent Support

They sat on the ground with him for seven days and seven nights. No one said a word to him, because they saw how great his suffering was.

JOB 2:13 NIV

Comforter, you see the cycles I go through with my grief. It seems like some days I am fine and others I can barely function for the sadness that overtakes my being. I know that you don't leave me; when I can't get out of the bed in the morning, there you are, closer than my blankets. When I am overcome by a wave of sorrow that cuts through every emotional reserve I had stored up, you surround me and hold me together.

I'm so grateful that you don't require me to be better than I am. Help me to remember that happiness does not equate to godliness. I am undone by my pain, but you are present in comfort and compassion. When I watch others go through the heaviness of grief, may I offer the comfort and support of being present and not requiring anything of them. What a wonderful example of comfort you've given me. I lean into your grace again today. I know you'll never fail in loving me well.

What has grief taught you about comfort?

Trust Him

"You have also given me the shield of Your salvation; your gentleness has made me great."

2 SAMUEL 22:36 NKJV

Holy God, you are the strong fortress that I run into in the storms of life. You are my shield and my protection; you have saved me with your faithful love. When I am tempted to go my own way and forge a path in the wilderness thinking I know best, would you redirect me to your path of life that is already present? You are what I need in every season; you are the wisdom I need to make decisions, the hope I need in the darkness of night, and the love that assures me of my intrinsic worth.

Thank you, God, that everything I have need of is found in you. Your presence is my source of life itself. When I am beaten down by the worries of this world, dragged down by the expectations of failure, and pulled under by waves of depression, would you be my victorious defender, saving me over and over again? I have given you my life, Lord, and I trust you to lead me on in your love.

What has helped you to trust God in different circumstances in life?

Perfect Power

"My grace is sufficient for you, for power is perfected in weakness." Most gladly, therefore, I will rather boast about my weaknesses, so that the power of Christ may dwell in me.

2 Corinthians 12:9 nasb

Gracious God, you are so lavish in love. Your strength is my source when I have no resources of my own left. Your Word says that your power is perfected in weakness; may I find this to be true in my life! When I am weak, then I am really strong because I am leaning into your power that is beyond anything I could muster up. While the rest of the world is bragging about their strengths, may I not fall into that trap. Instead, may I revel in the power you give in my weakness.

I am so limited, Lord. What a mystery that in your kingdom that actually is a benefit! Keep my heart humble in your presence that I would glory in your grace made evident in my life. Have your way in my frailty today.

How have you seen God's power make up
for your weakness?

Proven Character

We also have joy with our troubles, because we know that these troubles produce patience. And patience produces character, and character produces hope.

ROMANS 5:3-4 NCV

Lord, your incredible character is unchanging in its goodness. Your mercy who can fathom? Who can comprehend your mysterious grace? The abundance of your love cannot be measured, and your peace is not short-lived. God, in your constancy, you guide me in kindness and hem me in with compassion. May my heart know your consistent presence in every hardship, every trouble, every joy, and every celebration. You are the same through it all.

Point me back to the faithful thread of your mercy through the ages when I start to question whether walking in your way of love is worth it. When the road gets bumpy, I know that it is only for a stretch; smooth it out, even as we walk it together. May my heart be patient in awaiting the hope for which I am on this path to begin with. May I never lose sight of you.

How has your character grown through hardship?

Tended

He heals the brokenhearted
and bandages their wounds.

PSALM 147:3 NLT

Healer, you see my brokenness so clearly. Like a skilled doctor assessing their patient, you see what my condition is. Come close in your comfort and bind up my wounds. Heal me with your love. I rely on you to do it. When I am tempted to stay in my wounded state to keep the connection to my loss strong, would you give me a taste of your wholeness? May my memories stay intact as the pain associated diminishes. I trust that in my healing there will be sweetness where there was only agony before.

Lord, I'm so grateful that you tend to each of your children perfectly. You know just what each of us needs right when we need it. Today, I yield my own ideas of my needs and ask that you would meet me with what you know I need—what I don't even know to ask for. Heal me, and I will be healed.

Are you ready for God to heal your broken heart?

Tapestry of Grace

We are convinced that every detail of our lives is continually woven together to fit into God's perfect plan of bringing good into our lives, for we are his lovers who have been called to fulfill his designed purpose.

ROMANS 8:28 TPT

God on high, you are weaving a tapestry of your grace through all of creation. I know that my life is not untouched by your love. Today, give me eyes to see where you have been working all along. As I look back on my history with you, let me see your telltale love sewn into the fabric of my story. Even in areas where I had no idea you were paying attention, as I look back I see that you have been taking everything into account.

What a wonderful, attentive God you are. You are intricately involved in my life, weaving every part together into a beautiful masterpiece. I know that you won't let anything I go through go to waste; turn it all around for your glory. In the midst of darkness and heavy sorrow, you will knit your faithful love through it. You are incredible, and your attention to detail is astounding.

Where can you see God's mark of love as you look back on your life?

His Work

The LORD will fulfill his purpose for me;
your steadfast love, O LORD, endures forever.
Do not forsake the work of your hands.

PSALM 138:8 ESV

Lord, your faithful love is present every moment of my life. As the seasons shift and I look to the falling leaves as a cue that it's time to let go, I trust that you remain constant through every stage. May my heart find its confidence in your steadfast love that never ebbs. You are always overflowing with mercy; there is no low tide of your kindness.

Your love is more reliable than the rising sun. Don't forget about me, Lord. Don't make me persevere through the coming winter on my own. Don't leave me; I rely on the warmth of your presence to sustain me. Encourage my heart in your love and lead me on in your mercy. You will fulfill your purpose for me even if at times I lose sight of it. May I never lose sight of you.

Do you trust God to keep working in your life when you can't see the purpose?

Nothing Between

In all these things we are more than conquerors through Him who loved us. For I am persuaded that neither death nor life, nor angels nor principalities nor powers, nor things present nor things to come, nor height nor depth, nor any other created thing, shall be able to separate us from the love of God which is in Christ Jesus our Lord.

ROMANS 8:37-39 NKJV

Constant One, your Word is clear that nothing can separate us from your love. The passionate pursuit of your people is the hallmark of your love. It stops at nothing to chase us down. Today, I'm right in the pathway of the rushing tide of your love. In fact, I've been living in the boundaries of it for longer than I can remember. Nothing, absolutely nothing, can keep me from your affection.

And yet, here I am longing for a new revelation, a fresh encounter with this love that conquers every fear. Spirit of God, wash over me with wave after wave of the peace that passes all understanding. With your mercy as the fire burning in my soul, I will come out of every circumstance a victor because your love already won.

Are you convinced of God's powerful love overcoming everything you think could separate you from him?

Spirit Power

The Spirit of the LORD will rest on Him,
The spirit of wisdom and understanding,
The spirit of counsel and strength,
The spirit of knowledge and the fear of the LORD.

ISAIAH 11:2 NASB

Spirit of God, you are the strength of my soul. When I am weak, you empower me with the strength of your grace. When I lack knowledge, you bring the revelation of wisdom. When I am afraid, you surround me with the peace of your presence. When I am confused, you bring clarity. When I am grief-stricken, you are the comfort that holds me together.

In you, I find everything I need. I'm so grateful that your work in my life isn't just something I can recognize if I look closely. Your tangible love is evident in more ways than one; you fill my life with the fruit of your presence. I invite you to meet me with your power once again, here and now. In kindness draw near. I am open to you.

How have you experienced the Holy Spirit's power in your life?

Saturated

Let every activity of your lives and every word that comes from your lips be drenched with the beauty of our Lord Jesus, the Anointed One. And bring your constant praise to God the Father because of what Christ has done for you!

COLOSSIANS 3:17 TPT

Beautiful One, may I be saturated by your love today as you meet with me. I turn my attention to you, holy God. Flood my mind with your truth, calming the distraction of worries about the unknown. Bring peace to my body as I breathe you in. May all I do today be rooted from a place of confidence in your unfailing love. You are able to do more than I could ever imagine. Stir up hope in my heart again.

I won't hold back my thanks from you today. You have led me this far, and I trust you to continue to guide me in your goodness all the days of my life. There hasn't been a moment where your love lifted from my life, or even a second where you second-guessed your compassion. Your affection brings life to my bones and sets my soul on fire with purpose. I praise you because I am purposefully and wonderfully made!

How has God's beauty changed you?

Delivered Again

The righteous person may have many troubles,
but the Lord delivers him from them all.

PSALM 34:19 NIV

Lord, you are my deliverer. You save me from my troubles over and over again. Don't stop, now! Keep lifting me from the grips of death and despair. Don't let me be lost to confusion or doubt. Lead me in your faithful love and wisdom all the days of my life. When I hesitate to hope in you, you still follow through in faithfulness. Who else is there like you? You are not easily offended. Let my heart be woven together with yours: your love the thread, coated in trust.

Lord, you see the difficulty of persevering in faith through hardships, pain, and heartbreak. I'm so grateful that your faithfulness is not reliant on my own though you know how I long to stay close to you through it all. Encourage my heart in hope again. Lift my head to meet your gaze. Where I have become downcast and discouraged, give me the perspective of your viewpoint that brings relief and clarity. I hold onto hope that you won't ever abandon me.

How has God delivered you from troubles?

Led to Life

Godly grief produces a repentance that leads to salvation and brings no regret, but worldly grief produces death.

2 CORINTHIANS 7:10 NRSV

Patient One, your kindness leads me back to you time and time again. Nothing goes wasted in your love; even grief has found a purpose in calling me back to you. In my sorrow, I have no hope for healing or reconciliation on my own. I cannot heal my bleeding heart; I can barely stay conscious in my life for all the sadness seeping out of my soul. But you, Lord, you bind up the brokenhearted. You heal those overcome with the agony of mourning. You do. In the process of grieving, I will not forget that your love is powerful enough to fill every crack and crevice. You won't let me drown in sorrow.

In you there is hope. Hope for life beyond this small, lived existence. Where there is hope, there is light, and where there is light, there is life. I set my eyes on you again today, trusting you to do what only you can do.

In your grief, have you known God's kindness and restoration?

Have Mercy

Answer me when I pray to you,
my God who does what is right.
Make things easier for me when I am in trouble.
Have mercy on me and hear my prayer.

PSALM 4:1 NCV

Merciful God, you always do what is right. I don't have to wonder or worry about what I'll get with you; you are always generous in love and consistent in kindness. As I travel through this life, I depend on you in every season. You are my constant companion through it all. Be quick to answer me today as I call on you.

You have seen me through hardship and trials; you have been faithful through the joys, as well. Do not let me be discouraged today; I have turned my attention to you. Light up my life with the radiance of your glory. Let me know your wisdom in a fresh way. There is no problem too complicated for you, and there is no question I could pose that would stump you. Meet me in the nitty-gritty of my present reality and turn my day around. Bring hope and encouragement where I can't see any. You are so good—I wait for you to come through for me again.

Will you offer God the honest state of your heart today?

No One Else

No one is holy like the LORD!
There is no one besides you;
there is no Rock like our God.

1 SAMUEL 2:2 NLT

Yahweh, you stand alone in power. Your greatness is unrivaled and your power unmatched. Who else is there like you in all the earth? There is no one who could defeat you when they challenge your power. Though the weapons of this world are wielded with intimidation, the greatest force in the universe is your unfailing love. It conquered death and the grave—you proved that with the resurrection of Jesus.

What a wonderful God you are! Loyal in love, a strong and steady shelter for the weak, a constant help in times of trouble; that is who you are! There is no one else like you; no one can compare. I am so grateful to be known by the God of mercy who consistently reaches out in kindness and grace. I rely on you; I trust you won't ever fail!

What are some attributes of God that amaze you?

Shared Burden

If one part suffers, every part suffers with it;
if one part is honored, every part rejoices with it.

1 CORINTHIANS 12:26 NIV

Constant One, I look to you today for the strength I so desperately need. In your love, reach out and surround me with the peace of your presence. I know that I'm not alone. I'm so grateful to have your Spirit as my constant companion and comfort. You are the wisdom that keeps me in line. I also know that you have created us for community. May I not take for granted the people in my life who love you and love me well.

In my loneliness, may I not be lost in isolation. Help me to reach out for help even if it's just for a listening ear or a word of encouragement. A shared load doesn't feel as heavy; when my pride tries to keep me from asking for help, would you remind me that I was never meant to bear this alone? And when I am in a better place, may I be a willing and compassionate friend to those who need a shoulder or an ear. May I find strength in the camaraderie of community.

Who can you turn to for support in your loneliness?

Test It Out

Do not believe every spirit, but test the spirits, whether they are of God; because many false prophets have gone out into the world.

1 JOHN 4:1 NKJV

Great God, you are higher than the highest heights, and yet you are present in the details of my life. Your Spirit is with me in wisdom, guiding me according to your Word. May I not be quick to follow a line of thinking that isn't proven to be aligned with your unchanging character. As I measure the fruit of a word, I will be able to sift the life-giving nuggets from those that are like a millstone, dragging me down in shame.

God, I am grateful to know your nature and that you never change. As I look to the life of Jesus, I see how often the Pharisees mistook the law as a rigid rulebook rather than an indicator of your consistent nature. As I test what is behind different movements presented in my life, may I only align with the ones that reflect your nature and not the pride of man.

What is the measure you use to test whether a word is from God or not?

Counseled by Wisdom

I will instruct you and teach you the way you should go;
I will counsel you with my eye upon you.

PSALM 32:8 NRSV

Holy One, you are the one I look to in every season of life
for wisdom and discernment. As I journey through this
life, I look to you to guide me in your love and light. I find
wisdom as I take time to pray and consider which way to
go when a fork appears in the road. I won't worry about
whether to go right or left; I know that you are with me no
matter where I go.

I rely on your wisdom to advise me. You are the best
teacher I've ever known, and you empower me to make
choices according to what you have taught me. You
don't dictate my life like a micromanager; you give me
the freedom to choose, and you counsel me with your
knowledge and care. I'm so grateful that I don't have to
depend on my inadequate understanding; you are a wealth
of wisdom, always weighing in with powerful insights when
I come to you!

How has God's wisdom directed your life?

In Process

I pray with great faith for you, because I'm fully convinced that the One who began this glorious work in you will faithfully continue the process of maturing you and will put his finishing touches to it until the unveiling of our Lord Jesus Christ!

PHILIPPIANS 1:6 TPT

Father, you yourself breathed your life into my being in the beginning. My origin story goes back to you. You haven't stopped redeeming my life since I surrendered it to you. You work everything together in such a marvelous way—I can't see how all the details connect quite yet though I've seen enough to know that you are doing it. I know that you haven't given up on me; I trust that you are working under the surface of my life to sow and produce fruit that will last.

It is such a wonder that you never stop weaving your love into your children's stories. I am yours, Father, and I trust that in your goodness you will bring beauty out of even the most barren situations. You are so much better than anyone I've ever known. Continue to do what you're doing and give me glimpses of your goodness at work. Refresh my eyes and encourage my heart in you again today.

Do you trust that God is working in your life even when you can't see it?

Eternal Life

"God so loved the world that he gave his one and only Son, that whoever believes in him shall not perish but have eternal life."

JOHN 3:16 NIV

Unchanging One, my hopes are set on you. Everything that I desire is fleeting—my longings pass away, except for that which finds its home in you. Your love knows no limits, and it is this unfailing love that covers and carries me through every day of my life. Today, meet me with the mercy of your heart and love me to life. Let your light shine into the shadows of my soul, bringing clarity and peace.

In walking through grief and loss, the sting of death is real; I cannot pretend to not be gutted by the sorrow that mourning elicits. And yet, there is hope even in the grief. Though the awaiting reality of eternal life doesn't ease the separation of loss, it does bring hope to the journey of life. Lord, would you give me the peace that passes all understanding today as I set my eyes on you, the Eternal One?

Do you have the assurance of eternal life?

Capable

Using the Scriptures, the person who serves God will be capable, having all that is needed to do every good work.

2 TIMOTHY 3:17 NCV

Good God, I don't rely on my own strength to get through today; I need your grace to empower me to life. I am weak—so weak—but you are strong. I lean into your presence, inviting your mercy to fill me up with the fuel I need. Thank you that you did not leave me to guess at how I should live. In your Word, I find the guidance I need. In your Spirit, I have found the power I need to follow along your path of love.

Lord, as I go about my day, I invite you to interrupt my moments with your loving truth that compels me in compassion. May I not be so focused on myself that I can't see the needs of others around me. In all that I do, let me be attuned to your voice speaking your truth in every circumstance. Thank you for relationship that is fluid; I love getting to know you, even as I am known by you. What a beautiful exchange.

What truth has moved you to act in compassion?

Mandate

Bear one another's burdens,
and thereby fulfill the law of Christ.

GALATIANS 6:2 NASB

Lord, in following after you, I have found my purpose in your love. Your law is simple when it comes down to it; it is not complex. It is simple enough for a child to understand, and yet it is not an easy path. Your law of love requires that we consider others the way we consider ourselves— to choose love at all cost. When we bear one another's burdens, we love as you loved.

Lord, when I would rather build walls instead of bridges and hang on to offense rather than offer an olive branch, would you remind me what your love cost? There is not one who has earned your love; you offer it freely without condition. May I live the same way even when it is costly and the hardest thing I could do. May I offer forgiveness instead of rebuke, and may I love others even when it is inconvenient to do so. Love is so worth it.

What does it feel like to have a burden shared?

Continual Surrender

By the help of your God, return;
Observe mercy and justice,
And wait on your God continually.

HOSEA 12:6 NKJV

God, you are my help and my strength. I rely on you to even turn my attention to you; may the presence of your Spirit bring peace to the chaotic thoughts in my mind. Bring rest to the anxiety of my heart. As I wait on you, I contemplate your amazing attributes of lovingkindness and mercy. You are just and true; you do not deal falsely with some and in truth with others. You never lie, and you don't cheat; you are incredibly reliable in love.

I'm so thankful that you don't grow tired of extending mercy; some days it seems like I need it endlessly. Though I fall over and over again, you pick me up every time. I won't stop turning to you; where else can I find true acceptance and unbiased affection? You are truly the most amazing love I've ever known. May I be transformed more and more in your likeness. Here I am, right here and now; renew me as I surrender to you again.

Do you think you can weary God of his mercy?

Justice

The LORD waits to be gracious to you,
and therefore he exalts himself to show mercy to you.
For the LORD is a God of justice;
blessed are all those who wait for him.

ISAIAH 30:18 ESV

Righteous One, teach me how to be patient in hope and aligned in mercy. Your love is more constant than the fire of the sun, and your passion burns brighter. I rely on your kindness in every season of my life. You can't be talked out of your grace, and your heart of justice is set according to your mercy. Only you can judge, and only you have the wisdom to see through to the heart of every human. I trust you to do the judging; may my heart expand in your love.

As I wait on you, you surround me with your life-giving presence. You know what I need—what I don't even know to ask for. Meet me with your compassion and fill me with the light of your wisdom.

*Can you lay down your idea of justice
and surrender it to God today?*

Worn Down

LORD, have mercy, because I am in misery.
My eyes are weak from so much crying,
and my whole being is tired from grief.

PSALM 31:9 NCV

Compassionate One, when my soul is crushed by grief, and sorrow is the only emotion I can feel, would you surround me with the embrace of your presence? Comfort me with your kindness and relieve my weeping with your mercy. Give me reprieve from the weight of this sadness. I know that you hear me whenever I call out to you, and you won't delay in helping me.

Meet me with exactly what I need today. Give me grace where I am weak and be the strength that sustains me. Thank you for your constant presence that never abandons me in suffering; you don't need to take a break from the weight of my sadness. You help lift the weight of it as you sit with me. I lean into your love today as I do every day. When I am in anguish, your presence lightens the load. Come closer, Lord.

When you are worn down by grief,
have you known the relief of God's comfort?

November

Be faithful to pray as intercessors
who are fully alert
and giving thanks to God.

COLOSSIANS 4:2 TPT

Overflowing Mercy

The Living Expression became a man and lived among us! And we gazed upon the splendor of his glory, the glory of the One and Only who came from the Father overflowing with tender mercy and truth!

JOHN 1:14 TPT

Living God, your mercy is astounding in its intensity. You cover every weakness, lift off the shame of every failure, and you bring life to the most barren places. I know that you are overflowing with truth and that your love is stronger than death. Your compassion reaches out and tears down every wall that would keep me from you. In the resurrection of Jesus, every barrier was broken down. There is no more veil that keeps mere humans from God's presence. Your Spirit is with me, breathing life and working in miracle power.

Today, I am reminded of your overwhelming affection that stopped at nothing to pursue uninterrupted fellowship with your people. I am grateful to be known as yours; may my heart be encouraged in your love again today. Flood me with the sheer joy of your presence that sets my feet to dancing. May today be the day that the cocoon of my mourning turns into a dance floor.

When is the last time you felt unbridled joy?

Transformed

We all, with unveiled face, beholding as in a mirror the glory of the Lord, are being transformed into the same image from glory to glory, just as by the Spirit of the Lord.

2 CORINTHIANS 3:18 NKJV

Lord, you are the hope of my heart. As I behold your beauty and reflect on your goodness, I find that I am being transformed into your likeness. Your Spirit is my life-breath, and I am becoming more like you with every inhalation. As I breathe you in, fill my heart with the peace that passes all understanding. As I gaze on your glory, may my face reflect the light of yours.

Nothing goes to waste in your hands, and I know you are working in my life even in the midst of tragedy and sorrow. Help me to continue to press into you in every season of the soul. When life knocks me down, I look up to find you are already lifting me. Do not hide yourself from me as I look to you; I depend on you more than I can express.

Do you believe that God is transforming you even in the midst of sorrow?

He Hears

Blessed be the LORD!
For he has heard the voice of my pleas for mercy.

PSALM 28:6 ESV

Good God, every time I call out to you, you answer. There isn't a whispered prayer or a silent plea of my heart that goes unnoticed. You hear it all, and you don't delay in sending your help. Your Spirit is an ever-present comfort in my sorrow. You are my strength when I have none. You are the light that illuminates my path and the wisdom that leads me when I don't know where to go or what to do.

I won't stop turning to you no matter what. Here I am again with my heart open before you. My life is laid out like an offering; may your mercy meet me right where I am. Spirit of God, stir up hope and faith once again where the dust of disappointment has settled. You are still good—I believe it!

Will you lay out your heart before the Lord again today, trusting that he hears and answers?

Clothed in Love

Beyond all these things put on love, which is the perfect bond of unity. Let the peace of Christ rule in your hearts, to which indeed you were called in one body; and be thankful.

COLOSSIANS 3:14-15 NASB

Christ, as I set my mind on you today, fill me with your peace that pervades every anxious thought and brings calm to my soul. As I dress myself in your love today, would you cover every weakness and imperfection? You are my shield, concealing my frailty and vulnerability with your abundant mercy. May my spirit be united with yours in the communion of your presence.

Without you, my defenses are down and I have little to offer anyone, including myself. You have so much to offer in your generous heart of affection. I won't try to get through today in my own strength or with my own restricted resources. I drink from your fountain of mercy again, and I find refreshment and hope here.

Have you been relying on your own resources to offer others?

It Belongs to Him

Yours, LORD, is the greatness and the power
and the glory and the majesty and the splendor,
for everything in heaven and earth is yours.

1 CHRONICLES 29:11 NIV

Lord over all, all power and strength belong to you. You are full of glory, and you shine brighter than the sun in purity and affection. Everything in heaven and on the earth belongs to you—I belong to you. Lord, let my heart stay open to your sovereignty when I think that circumstances should turn in a different direction. When the storms of sorrow whip me around, may I find myself anchored in your unfailing love that never lets go.

When I can't understand the disappointments in life that cause me to question your goodness, may my heart be drawn back to you with your devoted mercy. Even though I don't have the answers, I trust your character more than my own expectations. I know that your ways are higher than mine, and your thoughts are full of wisdom. Even through the darkest and most painful circumstances, you sow seeds of life that bring restoration and redemption. I will trust you today with every hope and every letdown.

*How have you seen God bring redemption
out of the ashes of destruction?*

Medicine for the Heart

A joyful, cheerful heart brings healing
to both body and soul.
But the one whose heart is crushed
struggles with sickness and depression.

PROVERBS 17:22 TPT

Merciful God, you have seen the state of my heart in every season and through every trial and triumph. In times of joy and celebration, there seems to be so much to be thankful for. In times of sorrow and distress, it is much harder to find obvious things to be thankful for. But in the midst of heartbreak, your love is as present as it ever was. I find your goodness in the little things in life, like children's laughter, a genuine smile, and the fresh air hitting my lungs. I know when I look for clues that you are still with me, I will find them.

Lord, be my very close and present comfort. When I cannot lift the crushing weight of the searing loss in my life, I trust that you will do it. Bring healing to my soul as you lighten the heavy load of sorrow and sadness that has kept me down. Lift me up in your love as you pour the oil of mercy over my life.

What was the last thing that brought joy to your heart?

At a Loss

In the same way the Spirit also helps our weakness;
for we do not know how to pray as we should,
but the Spirit Himself intercedes for us
with groanings too deep for words.

ROMANS 8:26 NASB

Holy Spirit, I rely on your help to even translate the groans of my heart into words. You don't need my thoughts to be formed to convert them into prayer. You know what I need at all times, and I depend on you to come through when I don't know how or what to ask for. I'm so grateful that you don't wait for me to know what I'm feeling before you come close with the comfort of your presence.

As you understand and present my heart before the Father, would you do the same from the Father's heart toward me? I long for a fresh word of encouragement; I don't want to just hope that you are with me; I want to experience the light of your glory all around me. Don't let me down. Keep pleading my case!

When you don't know what to pray,
do you trust the Holy Spirit to present your case?

Real Rest

All who have entered into God's rest have rested from their labors, just as God did after creating the world.

HEBREWS 4:10 NLT

Prince of Peace, I look to you for the rest my soul so desperately needs. You have seen the torment and the turmoil that has been keeping my heart racing in circles. I cannot go on at this pace; I need the rest that only you give. Holy Spirit, breathe your peace into my conscious mind and calm my anxious heart. Let your tranquility fill my soul as you lead me beside still waters. Here in the quiet, may I find reprieve from the chaos of my life.

Lord, you see how worn out I have become. You know how I need you, and not just in this moment but in all of them! I have forgotten what it means to abide in your peace; remind me today, not just with words but with your soothing presence. You've done it before; I trust you to do it again.

When was the last time you really rested?

Covenant Promise

My covenant I will not break,
Nor alter the word that has gone out of My lips.

PSALM 89:34 NKJV

Faithful One, you always keep your Word. As I recall your promises over my life, and the waiting that is associated with them, I will not hold back from bringing them all before you again. When you make a vow, you always follow through on it. You do not lie, and you don't mislead your children. Today, even with my doubts and difficulties, I bind my heart in trust of you once again. I belong to you, and that is no small thing.

When you speak, you act. When you promise, you fulfill. It is not always as expected, in fact most times it isn't. But you are faithful, nonetheless. Even the arrival and subsequent life of the Messiah was a far cry from what the Israelites were expecting in their promised Savior. May my heart remain connected to yours in unwavering trust as my own expectations and hopes fail. You are always faithful and you always will be.

What promises are you holding onto today?

Abundant Goodness

How abundant are the good things
that you have stored up for those who fear you,
that you bestow in the sight of all,
on those who take refuge in you.

PSALM 31:19 NIV

Good Father, you have stored up abundant goodness for everyone who follows you. You won't hesitate to pour out your blessings on those who call on your name. I have taken refuge in you more times than I can count, and I'm certainly not done running into your arms. You are better than I have been at every turn, and I know your character never changes.

I rely on your love to carry me through the hard days and to be the source of my strength when I have nothing of my own to offer. I trust that you won't hold back your goodness from my life; just as I have seen you do before, I believe that I will continue to see your kindnesses poured out in my life. I depend on you!

What evidence of God's goodness is there in your life?

On His Mind

See, I have written your name on my hand.
Jerusalem, I always think about your walls.

ISAIAH 49:16 NCV

Great God, I can't fathom the length of your love or the never-ending well of your kindness. Who am I that you would think of me? Who am I that the Mighty God of the universe would know the details of my life? Yet you, perfect Father, have called me by name as your own. You are the very one who knit me together in my mother's womb. I was not an accident, and you never second-guessed the work of your hands. There is not a nation, a city, or a person who is overlooked by you. You are intricately involved in the matters of your children.

Father, I come to you today with the boldness of a dearly loved child. I won't hesitate to turn to you with all that I am and have. You're not afraid of my questions, and you're not intimidated by my emotions. What a wonderful truth: that you see me, know me, and love me through and through. Overwhelm me with the kindness of your affection today.

Do you believe that you are worthy of attention?

Ready Help

God, hurry to help me, run to my rescue!
For you're my Savior and my only hope!

PSALM 38:22 TPT

Savior, I depend on your help to get me through every hardship, every trial, and every overwhelming situation. See where I am today and the odds that are stacked against me. You are never worried by the things that I am; I rely on you to get me through this. When I have nowhere else to turn, there you are with power to persevere. You rise to my defense in ways I don't even know to ask about. You are so much better than my closest ally. You never fail!

Bring peace to my heart as I trust you to follow through on your promise of redemption. Turn it all around with your goodness. If mountains can be moved and the dead raised, then you can take my humble situation and lead me to life again. Let not my heart be discouraged or given to despair. You are my hope, God—my only hope! Don't fail me now.

How has God been your help in times of trouble?

Chosen

You are a chosen generation, a royal priesthood, a holy
nation, His own special people, that you may proclaim
the praises of Him who called you out of darkness into
His marvelous light.

1 Peter 2:9 NKJV

Mighty God, your unfailing love chases me down in every
season of life. I am reminded that I have been adopted into
a family with God's own name as a stamp of identity. I have
been marked by your love. You are my Father, my leader,
and my friend. It is almost impossible to understand what
this means, but I know that someday I will see it all clearly.
When heaven's shores are before me, I will know you fully
even as I am already fully known by you. There will be no
more mystery, no more pain, and no more anguish.

I am grateful to be found in the light of your kingdom here
and now. Shine your revelation on my mind and give peace
where there have been anxious questions rising within my
chest. Your wisdom is better than my own; I rely on you
as you call me out. Thank you for drawing me into your
beautiful, welcoming family. May I reflect your compassion
as I live for you.

How does it feel to have been chosen by God as his child?

Sought and Found

"You will seek me and find me
when you seek me with all your heart."

JEREMIAH 29:13 NIV

Father, I am seeking after you with all of my heart. I have no hope apart from you. I have seen evidence of your goodness in my life before; give me eyes to see where you are working now in the midst of heartache and sorrow. I have been found in your love more times than I can count. Let me now find you in the midst of this mess. You bring order to chaos and peace to disorder. I trust you to do it right here and now.

If I were to spend all of my life pursuing you, it would be worthwhile. It is a dance of the quest, for you have been pursuing me harder and longer than I ever could. But I won't stop looking for you; I know that you're not far away. I'm not chasing after a far-off ideal; you are right here, like a father playing a game with his child, easily found. I won't despair today, for here I have found my hope again in your presence.

What have you found to be true about God's character?

Stick It Out

Blessed is the one who perseveres under trial because, having stood the test, that person will receive the crown of life that the Lord has promised to those who love him.

JAMES 1:12 NIV

Lord my strength, everything I need is found in you. I have a little strength on my own, but the tenacity of my faith is from the mercy that empowers me to know you. You have revealed yourself to me through your unfailing love that washes over me. The power of your presence has been my sustaining grace in the face of all sorts of trials. With you as my companion, comfort, helper, and wise leader, I can face anything.

You are victorious in all things, and when this short life is over, I will stand face-to-face with your unfiltered glory. My heart both trembles and longs for that day. Keep me steady in you all the days of my life, and don't let me drift from your path of love. Lead me back to you every time I start to wander away.

What keeps you persevering when
you go through hard times?

Draw Near

I am praying to you
because I know you will answer, O God.
Bend down and listen as I pray.

PSALM 17:6 NLT

God, you are my close comfort. You draw near with your lovingkindness with more consistency than the phases of the moon. Hear me as I call out to you. Here is my heart with every burden and every care. You see the things on the surface, and you see what is hiding in the depths. It's all plain as day to you. Lord, meet me with your kindness and answer the cries of my heart.

May your presence wrap around me with comfort as I wait on you. I need you more than I can say. Don't delay today. Take the kernel of faith that I have and water and feed it until it grows into a strong tree. I won't stop turning my attention toward you or submitting my life to yours. You have been my only relief and reprieve from the troubles that have been hounding me. You are so good. Let my life be lifted out of the muck and the mire. Set my feet on solid ground once again.

Will you open your heart to God once again?

My Praise

Heal me, O LORD, and I will be healed;
Save me and I will be saved,
For You are my praise.

JEREMIAH 17:14 NASB

Lord, you are my praise today and every day. Meet me with your mercy that heals every disease. You are my very present help in time of trouble. Save me when it seems that there is no way out. You always know the best outcome, and you don't fail to deliver. You will keep every promise that you've made with the seal of your loyal love as the guarantee.

God, meet me in my weakness; touch my body and my heart with your healing oil and bring life and restoration to that which has deteriorated. Heal me and I will be healed. Save me and I will be saved. It is what you do, Lord; I depend on you for it. I know that you will not withhold your love from me; fill me with faith to take you at your Word.

How have you experienced God's healing in your life?

Move My Heart

Jesus, when He came out, saw a great multitude and was moved with compassion for them, because they were like sheep not having a shepherd. So He began to teach them many things.

MARK 6:34 NKJV

Good Shepherd, you are the one I look to for leadership in every season of life. You are compassionate in your care for me, and you never get sidetracked by my failures or distracted by my worries. I'm so glad that I can't convince you to be caught up in the details the way I am, trying to control what I can. You are so much better than that. Lord, teach me your ways, even as I walk through the valley of suffering.

Your wisdom is full of kindness. Come close in your compassionate comfort today and lead me in your love. May my heart be so full of your mercy that it moves me in the same kindness toward others. You are my supply and my guide. Without you, I am lost.

When was the last time you were moved with compassion for someone?

Here's My Heart

My child, give me your heart,
and let your eyes observe my ways.

PROVERBS 23:26 NRSV

Father, here I am, heart wide open before you. It's all yours. I know that your wisdom is better than my own; in my sorrow, I trust that you know better than I do what is for my good and benefit. Though you don't throw me into the fire, you are with me in it. You sustain me, and you get me through. You never leave me alone, not even in my suffering.

You, God, are closer than my flesh and blood, and you are more caring than my parents. I have tasted and seen your goodness in my life, and I trust that I will see it again. Give me eyes to see your tender love in my present reality; fill my moments with your grace that carries me through every hardship. I submit myself to you because your love is better than life.

When was the last time you granted God
full access to your heart?

If You Would

I begged the Lord three times
to take this problem away from me.

2 CORINTHIANS 12:8 NCV

Jehovah, you are God of your Word. You never turn back on your promises, and you are faithful to do what you said you would. Lord, when I ask for things that don't have an easy answer, may I not hold back from asking in faith. And in the process of waiting, work in my heart to trust you no matter the outcome. I know that you hear my cries, and I won't stop calling out to you.

I surrender my own ideas to your unrivaled wisdom. I know that you see the whole picture and you don't miss a detail. When things don't go the way I hope they will, I will still lean into your love and trust your kind nature. Even in the midst of heartache, you sow seeds of restoration. In the middle of my pain, you weave the thread of your comfort through my wounds and hold me together. I will trust you as I hold out hope for better days.

How do you respond when God answers differently than you had hoped?

Save Me

He will care for the needy and neglected
when they cry to him for help.
The humble and helpless will know his kindness,
for with a father's compassion he will save their souls.

PSALM 72:12-13 TPT

Merciful Father, I rely on you more than I can say. You see the needs in my life and the neglect that my heart has undergone. I cry out to you again today. I won't stay silent when my peace is on the line. I have tried everything I know to get better, but I'm still lacking. In your kindness, meet me in the middle of my current reality. You are my Savior and my help.

You are a compassionate and righteous Father. You pursue me with your lovingkindness all the days of my life. I turn my heart toward your light of love today; let me soak in the rays of your life-giving glory. Lift my soul with the hope of your endless mercy that chases after me. You are incredibly good, God; let my life be marked by your goodness, even in my helplessness.

In what areas do you need God's help?

Holy Helper

"The Helper, the Holy Spirit, whom the Father
will send in My name, He will teach you all things,
and bring to your remembrance all that I said to you."

JOHN 14:26 NASB

Holy Spirit, you are my constant comfort, holy healer,
wise teacher, and my strong help. You are a faithful friend,
always loyally loving me to life. There is no darkness in you.
The revelation light you bring to my mind brings clarity
where there was misunderstanding. Your peace calms the
fiercest emotional storms within me. The comfort you give
makes me feel seen, known, and understood. Your affection
makes me come alive to who I've always been and makes
the weaknesses dim in comparison.

With my eyes magnified on your goodness, my heart
fills with hope. You are so much better than any love I've
ever known. You are without blemish; your love knows
no stipulations. There are no hidden conditions to your
kindness. Holy One, continue to do what only you can do
and bring life to the barren parts of me. I trust you.

*Have you known the Holy Spirit's
incomparable help in your life?*

Cheered On

Since we are surrounded by so great a cloud of witnesses, let us also lay aside every weight, and sin which clings so closely, and let us run with endurance the race that is set before us.

HEBREWS 12:1 ESV

Holy One, as I set my eyes on you today, I am reminded that I am not alone in this life. Not only do I have the help of the God of the universe, but also the shared vision and heart of those who love you. May I be encouraged to keep going with the support of those who have gone through the fires of testing and come out the other side. Where I have been weighed down by the cloak of fear, I shrug it off, running ahead with your love as my strength and vigor.

I won't stay stuck in the cycles of coping today. Today is a new day to choose a different way. And I choose you, Lord. Even if I start slow, with a crawl, I move ahead with your wisdom as my guide. Surround me with your mercy again and help me find those who are running the same race to set my pace to.

Who in your life encourages you to keep moving forward in faith and love?

Big Picture

A thousand years in your sight
are like a day that has just gone by,
or like a watch in the night.

PSALM 90:4 NIV

Creator, all living things find their origin in you. You are the giver of life, and you do not hesitate to restore and redeem that which has been broken and lost along the way. You were the same in the beginning as you are today. You are unchanging in pure love, power, and mercy. Your kindness will continue all the days that are ahead, on into eternity. You never fail in following through on your Word. You don't rescind your promises or take away your help from those who depend on it.

Though in my life I have had an idea of the timeline I think everything should fall into, your infinite wisdom is undeterred when my own plans fail or take longer than I expect. May my hopes and dreams be rooted in your love and not in my own idea of how they should happen. Your ways are always better because you see the bigger picture. In setbacks, in disappointments, and in the reimagining of what I thought would be, I yield to your will and way. I trust that your goodness is as constant as it ever was or will be.

*When your plans are upset, how does that affect
the way you approach God?*

Sound Mind

God has not given us a spirit of fear,
but of power and of love and of a sound mind.

2 TIMOTHY 1:7 NKJV

Good God, I rely on your understanding over my own. My limited logic fails me, but your wisdom never disappoints. Where fear has taken hold of my heart, I invite your perfect love in once again. Overcome every anxiety and worry with your powerful peace and marvelous mercy. Where confusion has had me changing my mind like the shifting winds, would you bring the clarity of your truth?

Your power is made perfect in my weakness; this is no less true in my mind. Wash over my thoughts with your words of life that last. You do not change your mind, manipulate the ones you love, or leave me to my own defenses. I trust in your love to cover and fill in every crack of doubt. To know you is to find my place—to be known. I will not trust my own knowledge above yours. Wise One, teach and lead me into your truth.

What brings you mental clarity?

Keep Asking

"If in my name you ask me for anything,
I will do it."

JOHN 14:14 NRSV

Faithful One, you clearly see through all the veneer of my life and straight to the depths of my heart. I don't want to hold anything back from you today. So here I am, Lord, laying bare my thoughts before you once again. I tune into my own heart and invite you into the messes that I am sorting out. In the areas of waiting that I've grown weary of asking about, I will lift my voice once again.

You are patient and kind; I know that you won't ridicule anything that I care about. Here is my heart, Lord; come and have your way in me yet again. Would you bring order to the chaos and shine your light of clarity that cuts through the fog of confusion? Your love has laid a foundation of hopeful expectation. Where I have tried to manage my own disappointment, I willingly lay down my control and ask for your wise and perfect viewpoint.

Is there anything you are hesitant to ask God for?

Better Desire

They desire a better, that is, a heavenly country.
Therefore God is not ashamed to be called their God,
for He has prepared a city for them.

HEBREWS 11:16 NKJV

Father, you are the author of my life. You formed my being, first in your imagination and then with your artist hand in my mother's womb. You knew what you were doing when you breathed life into my lungs; I am no accident. What a wonderful reminder that you created me on purpose. Where I struggle to know my worth, would you remind me that it is in being loved and accepted by you? You will never change your mind about me; your affection toward me is unwavering.

Thank you, Lord, for leading me through this life. As I walk through the valley of the shadow of death, I cling to you. I know you won't let go of me. I follow along your path of love, my hand gripping yours until you lead me into the great unknown of the eternal hereafter. Though I only see in part now, I trust that in the fullness of your glory I will see everything just as you do.

*Have you surrendered your heart
to the one who loves you fully?*

Satisfied

Even lions may get weak and hungry,
but those who look to the LORD
will have every good thing.

PSALM 34:10 NCV

Merciful One, I raise my gaze to you again today. Your kindness meets me each new day; I know that today won't be an exception. Though sadness and grief have depleted my emotional resources and have made it difficult to find satisfaction in anything, you remain the source of every good thing. Even if it is difficult to conceive of experiencing unhinged joy again, I trust that the days of being content and satisfied in you are not over.

Meet me with your great affection, Lord. Wash over my mind with your peace and bring clarity. May my heart find rest in you—true rest that sleeps deep and trusts the one who holds me. Satisfy my soul with the goodness of your mercy and compassion. You are my comfort, my friend, and my confidant. I hold nothing back from you today.

*Do you see areas of your need in your life
that you can trust God to fill?*

Goodness in Store

> "No eye has seen, no ear has heard,
> and no mind has imagined
> what God has prepared
> for those who love him."
>
> 1 CORINTHIANS 2:9 NLT

Marvelous Lord, in you is the fullness of every expectation I've ever had. Every hope is set on you alone, for you always come through on your promises. Even in disappointment, I find that the lack is never in you but in my idea of what is right and good. I trust that you will lead me into goodness and that I will experience the light of life once again. Joy will not remain a distant memory. With thanksgiving, I will find it woven into each part of my story.

Your beauty is beyond my imagination; your kindness is sweeter than a child's laughter. Where my heart has become discouraged, give me a glimpse of your incomparable goodness. I know that you are better than I am. You are more faithful than the sunrise, more reliable than the shifting of the seasons, and more loyal than the most ardent admirer. Reveal yourself to me in a new way. I am desperate to know you more.

When was the last time you were pleasantly surprised?

Governed by Grace

Remember this:
sin will not conquer you, for God already has!
You are not governed by law
but governed by the reign of the grace of God.

ROMANS 6:14 TPT

Gracious God, overcome me with your goodness today. You are the hope that lifts my soul to trust you over and over again. You are before and behind me; you are all around and you are full of love. My heart needs a fresh touch today. Refresh me in your life-giving presence. Wash over my being with the waterfall of your grace.

Lord, I belong to you. Nothing directs my life but you. I will not be overpowered by the world's ways or by the despair of dashed expectations. You will not let me be restrained by limited logic or held down by other's beliefs about me or my life. You are so much better than my most thrilling moments of clarity, purpose, and freedom. I trust that you have me even in the midst of storms and trials. You are my sure thing; I hold onto you as you hold onto me.

In what ways can you see God's victory over your life?

December

The LORD is close to everyone
who prays to him,
to all who truly pray to him.

PSALM 145:18 NCV

Peace Here

"Glory to God in the highest, and on earth peace among those with whom he is pleased!"

LUKE 2:14 ESV

Wonderful One, as we enter the season of Advent, I am reminded of the incredible gift of your Son. Peace came to earth in the form of Jesus, who lived a blameless life of promoting your love, healing the sick, setting the captives free, and leading us back to the one who is abundant in mercy, acceptance, and purpose. I could not find a better love if I tried.

Where I have been filled with anxiety, meet me with your calming peace that brings clear focus and rest. Where I have been drained of hope and purpose, would you fill me once again with your kindness that awakens my heart to life? You are endlessly good, compassionate, and true. Your Word never fails. Today, may your peace be the atmosphere of my inner world. I rely on you for all things.

How does Jesus' life portray God's peace?

Welcomed In

> "All that the Father gives Me will come to Me, and the one who comes to Me I will certainly not cast out."
>
> JOHN 6:37 NASB

Lord, I come to you with my life again today. You said that you wouldn't cast out the one who moves toward you, so I trust that you welcome me in with your love. It doesn't matter how little or how much time has passed, you are still as warm in your acceptance of me as you were the first time I was met with your mercy. I won't hold anything back from you today.

There are no exceptions to your wonderful love; you always reach out in kindness. There is no debt or failure that you can't more than meet with your mercy. You are skillful in restoration and unstoppable in redemption. I know that as I look to you, I will see how you are weaving your faithful care through even the most terrible situations. Here's my heart, open before you. Heal me with your kindness and restore my hope in your affection.

Are you convinced that God will never turn you away?

An Open Book

All my longings lie open before you, Lord;
my sighing is not hidden from you.

PSALM 38:9 NIV

Faithful One, in my sadness and heartbreak, I know that
I have been keeping my distance in some areas. But you,
Lord, see to the depths of my heart. You see what I have
not dared to speak aloud. I don't want to pretend anymore.
Right here and now, I lay out my longings before you. You
see them clearly in any case. I invite you into each one; be
gentle with me, for you know how vulnerable I am.

You are such a caring and attentive friend. You are lavish
in love, and you never push me down; you constantly lift
me up. May I be lifted in your love again today. You have
access to every part of me. Work your miracle power in
my broken expectations and the questions that I've been
guarding in the corners of my heart. I have tasted and I
have seen before that your love is better than life. May
today be a new opportunity for your grace to empower me
to life yet again.

Will you invite God into the hidden parts of your heart?

Today

This is the day the LORD has made;
We will rejoice and be glad in it.

PSALM 118:24 NKJV

Holy God, I submit my heart again to yours. With the opportunity of a new day, I recognize that you meet me with your mercy every single moment. This is a clean start to know you more. You won't give me stale bread when I ask to be fed by you. Your love is always fresh, always relevant, and always exactly what I need. Even in my disappointments, I find that your love satisfies in ways I couldn't have imagined it would.

Lord, as I look to you right now, may my heart respond to your love the way a flower responds to sunlight, opening before you. May gladness fill my soul as I remember your incomparable goodness. I know that you don't just give me enough strength to survive. May your joy be the strength that fills me to overflowing. I will rejoice for the sunlight, the breath in my lungs, and for your love that has never left me even for a moment.

What can you thank God for today?

Highest Law

"Love the LORD your God with all your heart,
all your soul, all your strength, and all your mind."
Also, "Love your neighbor as you love yourself."

LUKE 10:27 NCV

Lord my God, I offer you the most costly sacrifice I have:
my life. May my life be marked by the love you pour over
me in abundance. I offer you my little love in return, with
all my heart, all my soul, all my strength, and all my mind.
You have access to every part of me. My whole being is
subjected to your mercy, and I would have it no other way.
As I live for you, I walk along your pathway of peace that
chooses compassion for others over my own comfort.

It is no small thing that the highest law of heaven and earth
is love. It is more powerful than death, more lasting than
the highest mountains, and it stretches further than the
sunrise to sunset. Where I have made your love small in
my mind, break open the revelation of your kindness that
heals, restores, and redeems.

What is the driving force of your life?

Abide

Let what you heard from the beginning abide in you.
If what you heard from the beginning abides in you,
then you will abide in the Son and in the Father.

1 JOHN 2:24 NRSV

Father, remind me of the truth of your love that captivated
me in the beginning. Your kindness is what drew me to you
in the first place, and your wonderful compassion washed
away every blemish and stain. Shame has no rights to my
story with your mark of mercy stamped upon my life. Lord,
let me abide in the abundance of your lovingkindness; may
the river of your life in mine carry me through the twists
and turns.

Holy Spirit, may the truth of the Father's good and perfect
nature be sewn into the very fabric of my being. When I am
firmly planted in you, I will not be easily swayed by the winds
of change that blow through my life. May my roots go deep
in your faithful mercy, drinking deeply of your kindness. You
are the source of all goodness both now and forever.

What truths are abiding in you?

Get Back Up

The godly may trip seven times,
but they will get up again.
But one disaster is enough
to overthrow the wicked.

PROVERBS 24:16 NLT

Holy One, it doesn't matter how many times I trip up, you are always there to catch me and lift me back up again. When I am discouraged by the turn of events in my life, would you prove your faithful mercy by bringing redemption and leading me in your wisdom? You never fail to guide me; even in the darkness of the blackest night, your love leads me. You are confident in your understanding; I don't need to worry whether you know the best way to go when I submit my life to you.

When I am humbled by failures and dashed expectations, would you lift me again with your loyal love? I know that nothing surprises you; your love needs no backup plan. I trust that no matter what comes or what I walk through, you won't let me be taken out. You sustain me through every storm and circumstance. Let your peace be my portion in every dark night. I rely on you.

How has God's companionship given you resilience?

Yours

"Whatever you ask in prayer, believe that you have received it, and it will be yours."

MARK 11:24 ESV

Faithful Father, you are perfect in love and steadfast in kindness. You don't give your children snakes when they ask for a meal. You don't play cruel tricks on us; you are neither vindictive nor fickle. You are always compassionate. Your mercy is a hallmark of your character, and you don't ever change. Would you breathe fresh hope into my heart as I lay out my requests before you? I know that you know better than I do what is best, and I submit to your will. But I also know that you delight in giving your children the desires of their heart.

Lord, today, as I offer you the longings and desires, I ask for your gentle love to sustain my dreams. I yield to your kindness, and I expect nothing but love and acceptance from this exchange. You are so good. I won't hold back from you. There's no need because I always have an open invitation with you. Here I am, Lord.

What would you ask for if you knew you would receive it?

Perfect Pattern

I want you to pattern your lives after me,
just as I pattern mine after Christ.

1 CORINTHIANS 11:1 TPT

Perfect One, may my life be aligned in your love. I offer you my heart as I look to your perfect example of surrender and authority. Jesus, when I look to your life for direction, what I see is astounding. You chose compassion over comfort, kindness over pride, healing over appearances, acceptance over tradition, and love over law. Who else is there like you? May my life reflect your character as I follow on your path of love.

I'm thankful for new moments and opportunities to choose differently; when I mess up, you cover me in your mercy and lead me on. When I extend forgiveness, it is a reflection of the endless compassion that you've offered me. I can certainly get on board with following after you. You are not caught up in religious dogma or theology; you made it simple. The choice to love at all cost in every circumstance is the way of your life, of the cross, and of your resurrection. There is no other way. I will follow you.

What does walking in the way of love look like?

Free from Guilt

There is now no condemnation for those
who are in Christ Jesus.

ROMANS 8:1 NASB

Jesus, you are my covering and my shield. My life is hidden in you. Where I fail and fall short on a consistent basis is covered by your grace. You don't offer a free pass for all my past rebellion and then start counting strikes once I'm "in." Your grace is offensive in its scope and marvelous in its impact. Lord, may my heart stay humble as I journey with you on your path of love. I am undone by the mercy that you so freely offer. I don't take it for granted, but even if I did you wouldn't stop its flow over my life.

Where I have felt the clutches of shame and guilt, would you loosen their grip? I am found in you, Jesus, therefore who can condemn me? May I not fall into the trap of self-condemnation. Your love covers that! Where I expect more of myself than I would ever expect of others, may the constructs of perfectionism be dismantled within me. Your grace is enough for all of it. Thank you for setting me free from every chain.

*Do you excuse shame and self-condemnation
as being godly?*

Courageous

"Have I not commanded you? Be strong and of good
courage; do not be afraid, nor be dismayed,
for the LORD your God is with you wherever you go."

JOSHUA 1:9 NKJV

Victorious One, all the strength and courage I require
comes from you. With your presence as my sustenance, I
have everything I need to face every circumstance. When
my heart quakes at the thought of unknown outcomes, and
my soul shudders at the troubles I can't see my way out of,
I trust that you are wise in leadership. You won't ever leave
me, and you're not intimidated or unsure of anything. I can
trust that you won't ever make me walk into an impossibly
hard situation alone.

You are so good to me! Today, my soul is reminded of your
constant kindness that is woven through my life. You have
been faithful through it all, and I know that you will continue
to be. Why would I let fear keep me from what is in front
of me when I know that you are my guide and my defense?
May my heart take courage in your very present help!

*With God as your companion and help,
what can you face today that you've been avoiding?*

Growth

Grow in the grace and knowledge of our Lord and Savior Jesus Christ. To him be glory both now and forever! Amen.

2 PETER 3:18 NIV

Lord God, I lean into your wisdom today. I know that you know better than I ever could in every situation and circumstance. In contrast with my lack, you are full of everything I need. May I grow in your grace and understanding as I continually surrender my life to yours. You don't need me to invite you more than once, but I need the reminder of the practice of turning toward you. You can have my attention today. Redirect my gaze when I am distracted by the details and you are working on the bigger picture.

I know that you are with me in everything I face. You are with me in the trials, the triumphs, and everything in between. You are so much better than I could ever dream of being; as I grow up in your love and your truth, may my life bear the fruit of your Spirit's work.

How can you measure your spiritual growth?

Still Trust

When I am afraid,
I will put my trust in you.

PSALM 56:3 NLT

Faithful One, though I wish I could walk through this life without fear affecting me, it's just not my reality. I won't despair when fear floods my system; rather, I'll turn to you even in the midst of anxiety. The psalmist didn't say, "Instead of being afraid, I will trust you." He said, "*When* I am afraid, I will put my trust in you." In the same way, when fear closes in, I will choose to trust you.

Today, may the chorus of my heart be "I trust you." A thousand times over, may I choose it. You are so faithful and good, Father. I do not have to question whether you are with me; you have already promised never to leave or abandon me. You are with me in the joy and in the pain. As I choose you over and over again, strengthen me in your grace and love. I know you won't fail me.

What areas of uncertainty can you
choose to trust God with today?

Healed

"Behold, I will bring to it health and healing,
and I will heal them and reveal
to them abundance of prosperity and security."

JEREMIAH 33:6 ESV

Healer, meet me with the power of your presence again today. You have been my sustainer through the storm of loss and sorrow. You have been my redeemer in the depths of the darkest valleys, causing life to grow through the cracks and crags of the stony landscape of grief. You are my restorer, the one who is rebuilding my life from the ruins of broken dreams. Revive my heart in your love.

Lord, you have been my security in the midst of trauma; you have been the foundation of grace beneath my feet. I offer you every place that needs your healing touch. Release your power in my life and align me with your loving intentions for abundance and peace. I won't lose hope, for you have never let go of me or looked away from my suffering.

What areas do you need God to shore up with healing?

Mindset

Think about the things that are good and worthy of praise. Think about the things that are true and honorable and right and pure and beautiful and respected.

PHILIPPIANS 4:8 NCV

Mighty God, I set my mind on the things of your kingdom. I look for your goodness sewn into the details of my life like a pirate looks for treasure. You place evidence of your kindness in front of my eyes—your love is everywhere. I know that I won't stop finding your gracious fingerprints all over my story. Lord, today I trade in my sorrow for your joy. Your presence gives me life as I meditate on your lasting love that has not lifted from my life even for a moment.

Lord, as I focus my attention on your goodness, my heart can't help but respond with relief. I won't hold back my praise from you; your love outshines every other! Thank you for the good news of your faithful compassion that creates beauty out of the ashes of hardship. You are indescribably wonderful.

What have you been focusing your attention on?

Motivation

Every man's way is right in his own eyes,
But the Lᴏʀᴅ weighs the hearts.

Pʀᴏᴠᴇʀʙs 21:2 ɴᴀsʙ

Lord, here is my heart before you. Instead of trying to hold myself together today, I entrust myself to your qualified hands. Heal me with your love that I may be whole in you. Lead me with your wisdom through the questions and the quandaries. You are skillful in solving the most complicated problems. When I am tempted to run over my own questions with the guise of grace, meet me in the mess of my doubt. You are not afraid of my misgivings; I won't hide them from my own eyes or yours today.

You see straight to the heart of every matter, Lord, and you have a clear view of my every motivation. Align me in your love today; may your presence be the plumb line that reveals your true nature. Your abounding mercy is with me even now, seeping into the cracks of my soul. Lead me on in your love today and always.

Do you think you know better than God what's best for you?

Blessing

"The LORD bless you and keep you;
the LORD make his face shine on you
and be gracious to you;
the LORD turn his face toward you
and give you peace."

NUMBERS 6:24-26 NIV

Lord of my heart, lead me on in your love. Keep me steadfast as I follow you. Light my path with the radiance of your face; be gracious when I am lacking in faith. Turn to me when I call on you; let me see the fire in your eyes. How they burn with compassion, piercing the depths of my soul. Calm my heart with your plentiful peace and smooth the road out before me as I walk in your way.

There is so much unknown in life; in my quest to control, I've lost all vision for the best being outside of my own design. You are adept at making masterpieces out of shards of the mundane. You take the rubble and trash and rebuild it into something beautiful. Nothing goes wasted in your hands; you are a master maker, finding use and beauty in all things. I trust myself to your capable artistry.

What aspect of life can you stop trying to control today?

Father's Help

Give us a Father's help when we face our enemies.
For to trust in any man is an empty hope.

PSALM 108:12 TPT

Father, you are the help I rely on when my life gets overwhelming. You always know exactly what to do in every situation, and you fight for me when I don't know how to fight for myself. Your loving care of me is beyond my understanding, and I am so grateful to be your child. Why would I trust in my own reliability or even those around me when I know we will all fail.

Unlike my own resources, yours never run dry. You are full of wisdom for every circumstance and you have solutions for every problem I face. May I never wait too long to come to you for aid when I need it. Surely you will come through—you always do. My hopes will be fulfilled if they all depend on you. Fill me with courage as I walk hand-in-hand with you into the unknown of my day. Cover my weakness with your incredible strength as I lean into you.

What area do you need your Father's help in today?

No Comparison

I consider that our present sufferings are not worth comparing with the glory that will be revealed in us.

ROMANS 8:18 NIV

Good Father, when I walk through dark valleys, you are the hand that holds me and guides me through. As I experience the suffering of grief, I know that it won't be as debilitating as it has been forever. I trust that the solace I find in my sorrow is producing fruit that I will see later. Lord, give me a heart that holds onto hope even when I feel the depths of loss. Cover me with your compassion when I am overcome by grief.

One day, when all is made clear, I know that I will see what you were doing in the midst of the harshest of circumstances. Let me see how you are sowing seeds of beauty into the ashes of destruction. You are life-giver, and I know that character trait never stops. You renew, you restore, and you rebuild. May the redemption you bring blow every possible expectation out of the water.

Can you see where God has left kernels of kindness in your present reality?

Gift of God

By grace you have been saved through faith;
and that not of yourselves, it is the gift of God;
not as a result of works, so that no one may boast.

EPHESIANS 2:8-9 NASB

Gracious God, it is your work in my life that has any lasting effect. My own motivations and strength eventually wane, but yours never do. I'm so thankful that my salvation is not based on my own abilities but on your undying love. I never need to earn your love—you always give it freely. I run again into your arms of grace today. In your arms, I find a safe place to rest. You restore me as I lean into your love.

I have gladly received your gift of life through the grace that you give. I know that all goodness in my life is from you; I won't overlook what you have given me. May my eyes be focused on your kindness, looking for clues of your tender love planted in my life. Give me eyes to see how you are present with me.

How have you been trying to earn God's love?

A Father's Compassion

As a father has compassion on his children,
so the Lord has compassion on those who fear him.

PSALM 103:13 NIV

Perfect God, you are so attentive in tender love. Let my heart be opened more to your affectionate care today. May my mind receive the revelation of your very present goodness in my life. It is such a wonderful gift that I am not only known by you, but that I always have access to you through your Spirit. I come freely before you again with all that I am and all that I lack today. You are the peace that my heart longs for and the steady assurance that I need to keep following after you.

When I begin to forget your tender kindness, would you draw me back to you with your gentle touch? As you surround me with your loving embrace, I find that your unchanging love is always the answer to my restless heart. You are healing to my bones and hope for restoration. You rebuild as you weave your goodness into my hurting heart. I know that your strength is like a cord within my heart, pumping love from your heart into my own. I rely on you all the days of my life.

*When you think of God as caretaker,
does his kindness come to mind?*

Humble Love

Love is patient, love is kind. It does not envy,
it does not boast, it is not proud.

1 Corinthians 13:4 niv

Lord, you are full of unfailing love that knows no competition. Who else can claim that they love as purely as you do? I have never known a love like yours, that keeps no record of wrongs. You don't ever hold any of my sins against me. You don't hold onto grudges. I'm so grateful for that. Let me be full of this kind of love that changes from the inside out. A love that does not toot its own horn, is not exclusive, and doesn't resent anyone for what they do or do not have. Your love is purer than refined gold, kinder than the most affectionate mother, and patient beyond measure.

Truly, Lord, my mind cannot understand the scope of your affection. Enlighten my mind with the revelation of your love meeting me right here, right now. You have humbled yourself in love, never withholding your compassion when I seek it. Here I am, longing for more of you. I want—I need—to know your love in tangible ways in my life. Don't hold back now.

*When you consider the attributes of love,
how does your heart respond?*

Perfect Timing

For everything there is a season,
and a time for every matter under heaven.

ECCLESIASTES 3:1 NRSV

God over all, in you everything finds its fulfillment. I cannot pretend to have it all together or know what tomorrow will bring. In this tumultuous season of grief, my expectations have been pummeled and reset countless times. What I wish I could do I don't have the capacity for. What I want to be for others around me I have no strength to be. That has been a hard pill to swallow. You are not surprised by any of it. You haven't put unrealistic expectations on me. I have had to readjust my own beliefs about myself too many times to count. I'm tired of being at the end of my rope.

Lord, shift my perspective today. Let me see from your lens of love that takes everything into consideration and doesn't miss even the minutest detail. Lift the burden of what would be normal expectations over myself and others, calming my mind with the reality that you accept me in the state I'm in. You are patient and kind; let that rub off on me as I practice extending both patience and kindness to myself in this season.

How can you readjust your expectations of this season?

Wonderful Counselor

A child has been born to us; God has given a son to us.
He will be responsible for leading the people.
His name will be Wonderful Counselor, Powerful God,
Father Who Lives Forever, Prince of Peace.

ISAIAH 9:6 NCV

Emmanuel, you are God with me. Your presence is constant—what a wonderful gift! Thank you, Father, for the gift of your Son, Jesus, who ushered in the Holy Spirit's reign until we are united as one with you in the age to come. Everything that we have been taught about you is made evident in the life of Jesus and in the Holy Spirit's power alive in us now. It is too much to truly comprehend, and yet the taste of your goodness among us is sweeter than honey.

This holiday, my heart needs your very present comfort. There is a fresh wave of sadness as I face this joyful season with the sorrow of loss. I'm so grateful that I don't have to pretend with you. You are the Wonderful Counselor, and you are my Prince of Peace. Flood my heart with your peace again today, so as I grieve, your presence would be the sweetness I long for. Be a healing balm over my broken expectations.

What emotions does this holiday season evoke in you?

Messiah

"Today in the town of David a Savior has been born
to you; he is the Messiah, the Lord."

LUKE 2:11 NIV

Son of God, you are the fulfillment of God's promise to
send a Messiah to save his people. What a wonder that
you put on flesh and bones and humbled yourself to the
broken human experience. And yet, the world never knew
anyone like you. In your life, you commanded sickness to
leave bodies, breath to return the dead to life, and stormy
seas to calm. You spoke with authority, lived in humility,
and offered your very body as a sacrifice to break the
bondage of sin and death. Your tender affection for those
society looked down upon revealed the love of the Father.
Your choice of friends revealed that the Father was never
looking for the perfect or qualified to reflect his love.

In your living, Jesus, you showed us that the Father really
does delight in mercy. In kindness, you never excluded
people from your gatherings. In your dying, you showed
the lengths that love would go to tear down every wall that
kept people from knowing you. In your resurrection, you
revealed that your power transcends the grave and death
is not the end. It is that power that I look to today to fill me
with hope for life ahead.

How does Jesus' life fill your heart with wonder today?

Overflow

"He who believes in Me, as the Scripture has said,
out of his heart will flow rivers of living water."

JOHN 7:38 NKJV

Generous God, I stand under the waterfall of your grace
and goodness today. You are a pure spring feeding rivers
of living water that flow over your creation. As your child, I
know that you won't hold back your love from me. Fill me
to overflowing, that as I go about my day, your love would
flow freely my life. I've been running on low for far too
long; let today be a new day full of refreshing that brings
hope and joy.

God, I look to you like you are the only one that matters.
I set my mind and my attention on you; my heart is
confident in your goodness. Let no lesser love distract
me from your abundant kindness that is offered every
moment. I won't turn away from your mercy today; let my
heart overflow with your compassion toward everyone I
encounter, myself included.

*When was the last time you felt like you were being
carried down the river of God's grace?*

Forgiveness

"If you forgive those who sin against you, your heavenly Father will forgive you. But if you refuse to forgive others, your Father will not forgive your sins."

MATTHEW 6:14-15 NLT

Merciful Father, may my life be aligned with your heart of love. As you have forgiven me, may my heart also choose to pardon those who have wronged and hurt me. I realize that often the offense I feel is hurt that has nothing to do with the other person—it is pressing on a wound from long ago. Help me to know when to forgive and let go and when I should forgive and reconcile. I know that as I follow your example, I will find my way.

Holy Spirit, you are my help in this and all things. I rely on you to lead me in love and understanding. When my heart is struggling to hold onto offense, would you show me the root of it? Heal the heart wounds of my past and give me perspective to be able to let go of the resentment that eats away at my joy. I know that as I choose to follow you in this even when I don't want to, I will find freedom and your goodness awaiting me.

Who do you need to forgive today?

Great Confidence

The LORD will be your confidence,
And will keep your foot from being caught.

PROVERBS 3:26 NASB

Lord, may all the conviction in my heart be rooted in you and your unchanging nature. You faithfully follow through with everything you said you would do. Your promises will be fulfilled; every intention that you have set forth into this world will find its place. When I don't know what to hold onto, I hold onto you. When I don't know who to trust, I trust in you. Though I am confident in my own abilities to a point, I am incredibly limited in my scope of capability. But with you, nothing is impossible.

When I look at my life and see the question marks over my future, I know that they are not questions to you. You see the end from the beginning and know just what choices will be made along the way. I know that your intentions for me are good, and that, above all, you are with me through it all. You are not worried about what will come. May my heart rest in the confidence of your mercy and unfailing love that is present with me in every moment along the way. There is no need to give into fear when you are my constant companion and wise guide.

Where does your confidence lie?

Making Things Right

After you suffer for a short time, God, who gives all grace, will make everything right. He will make you strong and support you and keep you from falling. He called you to share in his glory in Christ, a glory that will continue forever.

1 PETER 5:10 NCV

Gracious God, I cling to you in my suffering and in my victory. In every season, every mood, and every circumstance, you remain the same faithful God. You are always abundant in compassion and generous with your affection. When I call to you, you don't tell me to wait for five minutes. You are with me whenever and however I need you. You are a perfect Father, a faithful friend, and the most caring comforter I've ever known.

When my feeble strength wanes, Lord, be my support. Hold me up when I'm falling, and grab hold of me when I feel like I'm slipping away. You are loyal in love; you won't let go. As I look and see the suffering around me, my heart is rooted in the expectation of your goodness. You will make everything right, and everyone that is relying on your power will be satisfied in your justice. Rebuild and restore and fill my heart with hope.

How has God supported you in your grief?

Wisdom's Instruction

Teach us to number our days,
that we may gain a heart of wisdom.

PSALM 90:12 NIV

Holy One, you are full of wisdom; you share your heavenly insights with those who look to you for help. Here I am again, asking for your perspective to be my guide. There are endless opportunities to choose to lean into your understanding over my own. In the mundane of the everyday, I get the opportunity to turn to you. I don't want to rely on my limited intellect; instruct me in your perfect ways.

I have seen how short life is, and the number of our days is surely unknown to each of us. I could be here one day and gone tomorrow as far as I know. May I live wisely with the brevity of life in mind. I submit my will and my ways to you, knowing that only what is from you lasts forever. Just as your love has no end, so there is always hope. Fill me today with the hope of a future whether it is in this life or the next.

When you consider the unpredictability of life's length, how does your heart respond?

A Fresh Start

"Behold, I am doing a new thing;
now it springs forth, do you not perceive it?
I will make a way in the wilderness
and rivers in the desert."

ISAIAH 43:19 ESV

Rebuilder, I commit my heart again to you today. I am hemmed into your love, constantly surrounded by you. I set my intentions on you as I look to a new year. I trust you as you continue to rebuild my life on the foundation of your mercy. I have walked through pain and darkness, but you have been with me through it all. As I look back, I see the fingerprints of your kindness though in the moment I struggled to see any evidence of your goodness.

You are so much better than my hopes could attest. I trust that when I am standing before you when I have stepped beyond this short life into eternity, you will reveal even more glory than I could anticipate. You are my greatest treasure, Lord. Lead me on into your goodness all the days of my life. I am yours!

How does the idea of a fresh beginning make you feel?